A World Alive

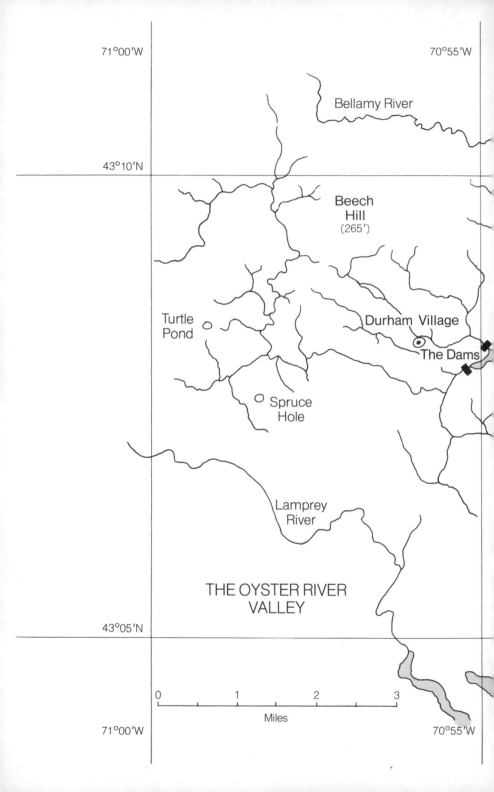

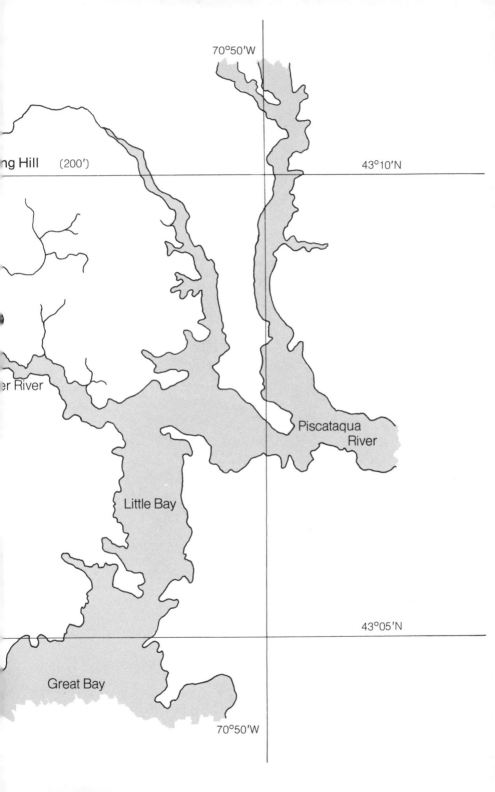

A World Alive

The Natural Wonders of a New England River Valley

Lorus J. Milne and Margery Milne

Photographs by the Authors,
Esther Heacock, and Fred Bavendam
Drawings by G. Don Ray

New Hampshire Publishing Company
Somersworth
1977

Library of Congress Catalog Card Number 76-55521
International Standard Book Number 0-912274-69-7

New Hampshire Publishing Company
Somersworth, New Hampshire 03878

All photographs by the authors except those
on pages 61, 84, 121, and 150, courtesy of
Esther Heacock; and on pages 16 and 46, courtesy
of Fred Bavendam

Printed in the United States of America

*To our many good friends in the valley,
especially Jeanne and Bill*

Contents

Illustrations

Prologue

Every glittering pearl of dew, or snowflake, or pelt of rain, conceals energy from the sun. Such energy sculptured the Oyster River valley of New England and most other valleys in the world. From the sun each day come the calories required to free molecules of water into an invisible vapor, to be randomly distributed by wind. The molecules again condense, and gravity propels the moisture through the soil, eventually to trickle out of springs into the deep reaches of the river. The water and the sun together nourish the plants of the valley; the plants, in turn, yield their bounty to animals and man. From one to another the energy goes, linking the living things together in countless ways.

The bonds linking plants, animals, soil, air, and mankind are essentially the same anywhere on earth. Only the creatures and perhaps the people are different, and their slight differences confer individuality. Now that we have lived among those of our valley for more than twenty-five years, we see how well they represent the whole of life.

This conclusion has been reached after traveling over all continents except Antarctica, and into some of their wildest parts. The world outside one's door is as fascinating a community as can be found. The commonplaces that everyone can see, whether trees or animals or fields or water denizens, provide a perennial joy and consolation. As William Morton Wheeler once noted, living things "are our only companions in an infinite and unsympathetic waste of electrons, planets, nebulae, and suns." Everything we learn about these companions adds to our own delight in life.

Since we first wrote this book, change has come to the Oyster River valley, and we will have something to say about that in the Epilogue. Of interest to bird-watchers, perhaps, is the fact that the American Ornithologists Union has decreed that the sparrow hawk (discussed on page 75) shall indeed be called the kestrel. And the northern yellowthroat (page 117) is now known as the common yellowthroat. The cardinal and the mockingbird have now become valley residents.

L.J.M. and M.M.

Durham, New Hampshire,
in the Oyster River valley,
September 1976

A World Alive

The Valley

All night the damp air moved inland, westward over the bay. Never shifting rapidly enough to swivel a weather-vane, by morning it had filled the whole valley to its low rim with a dense fog. From the upper surface of the heavy mist the rising sun flashed back into the sky. Yet its first warmth did not dispel the cloud.

A pilot from the nearby airbase noticed the shining mass of fog as he banked his jet fighter over the bay and whished inland at six hundred miles an hour. Care-fully he throttled back. This morning he had no need to break the sound barrier, thereby creating a twin shock wave that would jar people still asleep in the village and surrounding countryside, eight thousand feet below. He watched the contours of the compact cloud on the ground during the thirty-nine seconds his craft took to dart the six and a half miles along its greatest

1

dimension. He saw its edges folding and wrinkling along the valley rim. It was as though the cloud clinging to the dark land like a white ameba had a life of its own.

Ten minutes and a hundred flight-miles later, the pilot flew back over the same area and looked again for the cloud. Two parts remained, one small and circular, the other larger and oval. Half had vanished, exposing to the sky a bit of New England he knew as intimately as the switches and dials in his cockpit. There rose the school he had attended, and there the shining steeple of the community church. He could trace the familiar boundaries of the valley he had tramped so often. Through clumps of trees he caught glimpses of the tributary streams which combine to form the Oyster River. The steady glitter of water spilling over the dam, like a hyphen in white ink, caught his attention. Although short, it was straight—just as roads and runways were, or as were so many other evidences of the hand of man in the valley.

Below the dam, the larger bit of white cloud filled the estuary and also the beds of half a dozen lowland streams flowing a short distance into it. The smaller patch of fog, near the southwest corner, puzzled him for a moment. Then he recognized the white dot as fitting the steep declivity of Spruce Hole. He thought of the afternoons when he had pretended he was in an alien land as he explored the mysterious peat bog at its bottom. By forcing his way between the dwarfed black spruces, he could find rosettes of pitcher plants, whose strangely shaped leaves caught and digested insects.

Far more often he had hiked along the north shore of the estuary, and he could visualize it now under the dissipating fog. Probably the same great blue herons

2

were standing in the shallow water—waiting, waiting to stab down at lightning speed and impale a fish on their long beaks. When disturbed, they would complain with one squawk of alarm as they spread their broad wings and flapped ponderously off across the water toward the bay.

Where did the herons go around the bay shores? Often he had longed for wings, so as to follow the birds and learn the answer. Now that he did have the ability to fly, his pace was too swift, his altitude too great. He felt no nearer to solving his boyhood question than while standing on the ground. From the airplane he could not be sure whether the tide was coming in or going out, or even how low it was. Where did herons spend the hours of high tide? Perhaps they circled and settled in the marshes farther up the river, where they could catch frogs and beetles as well as different kinds of fishes. Why were there no frogs and beetles for the birds around salt water? He had no time to think about them now, for already he had entered the first leg of his own landing pattern. Switching on the radio transmitter, he called the control tower at the airbase, requesting brief exclusive use of a mile-long runway. There he set down his wheels—still at a speed faster than any bird ever flew.

The salty end of the Oyster River valley affords a landing field and hunting ground for herons and gulls at most times of day. It offers them good visibility too; there they can see in all directions, as well as be seen. The estuary still produces a few of the shellfish for which it was named in pioneer days. Yet, by comparison with the rest of the valley, it seems to have little significance. Most of the territory within the low rim of hills tilts obviously toward the fresh waters of the river. Its branching course

3

and the ponds along its length provide a focus for the valley. The estuary in the southeast corner seems merely the portal through which slow-moving night air so often brings a morning fog.

The irregular lobes in its outline give the Oyster River valley something of the shape of a big oyster, with the village at its center. A person can walk the length and breadth of the valley in a single day. But if he keeps his eyes open, he can see something new and different on every trip. Not that the valley's shape changes, for it has altered little in this respect since the Ice Ages ten millennia ago. Rather, its living things are in a constant state of flux, responding to little changes in the weather, to each other, and to the works of man.

Few of these changes can be detected from an airplane, although it offers the only vantage point from which the whole valley can be seen at once. But people on the ground notice, if they will, the details of change—details that can be compared with memories or records of what went before. In New England some of these records take the form of old stone walls and crumbling foundations hidden from the sky by clambering woodbine and honeysuckle, or by a canopy of trees. A walker in the woods, perhaps following some half-abandoned fire lane, can realize with astonishment how few decades the wild things need to take over farms of an earlier day.

Most of the animals stay silent and motionless while a walker passes by, and are overlooked. Yet they are watching and listening, well aware of his progress along the path or between the sapling trees. A pair of red squirrels may churr if their woodland privacy is invaded. Their ancestors probably planted the acorns and nuts from which the oaks and hickories grew.

4

A breeze sets the foliage shaking on a gray birch that sprang up in a saucer-shaped depression seven feet across, left by a forest giant that toppled during a hurricane. At one side of the depression are the uptilted remains of spreading roots which once filled it, supporting the great tree whose moss-coated trunk now lies partly buried in the ground. One bit of bark has resisted the agents of decay, and from it we recognize the toppled tree as a sugar maple. Perhaps a century earlier, a gentler wind brought to that same spot the winged seed from which the maple grew. Like pines and birches, elms and ashes, the maples rely upon the breeze. In springtime it carries their fragile pollen throughout the valley. Later it transports their progeny, as embryo plants needing only to fall on suitable soil. If it were not for the wind, how much of the abandoned farmland would now be covered by trees?

All of the valley that has been left undisturbed for a few decades is becoming forested. This change is predictable wherever the wind regularly brings to a temperate or a tropical land more rain and snow than it can carry off again as evaporated moisture. The surplus sinks into the ground and emerges in springs of pure water. From these it runs over the surface, as it does down the Oyster River, and provides a home for countless kinds of living things. It floods out into the estuary and becomes a lure for eel and smelt, a place for eelgrass and brant, a nursery habitat for countless ocean-going fishes and for shellfish.

So many seedlings have thrust upward from the moist soil to meet the energy coming from the sun that in a forest there is little room for new ones until the present occupants disappear. The surplus seeds, however, are

5

rarely wasted; they nourish a host of mice and insects, without which foxes and owls would go hungry. A ton of seedlings that find a roothold, only to be eaten, become the food for production of a hundredweight or so of deer, which otherwise might starve. All of these creatures finally join the fallen trees in yielding to the processes of decay, which unlock the heaps of raw materials needed in fashioning new life. Of these materials too the earth has a limited supply.

In many ways, the ponds and streams form a counterpart of the woodlands. They harbor a full assortment of different kinds of life, all exploiting the aquatic habitat and interacting with one another. Countless numbers of them drift in the upper water of each pond and slow-moving reach of the river. Mussels filter them from the water. Tiny water fleas and other minute crustaceans kick their way among the microscopic plants, capturing one after another at such a rate as to double their own numbers every few days if left unhindered. Small fishes, including sticklebacks, dart after the crustaceans. Game fishes, such as bass and pickerel, snap up the smaller fishes. Thus, step by step, the drifting algae in the water are transformed into food for an otter, a heron, or a kingfisher. Together, all of these hungry creatures keep the green plants from filling the pond. As on land, death and decay in the water furnish space and materials for new life.

Today the greater part of the Oyster River valley is occupied by neither woodlands nor water. It is in meadows and orchards, some of them abandoned as agricultural land only a few years ago. A meadow in New England is usually a man-made clearing, an area from which the trees have been cut, letting sunshine reach the

6

ground. It developed from a pioneer counterpart of to-day's level airbases, such as the one on which the jet pilot landed after his brief journey over the valley. If the airbases are abandoned, they too will become meadows.

Whenever farmlands or airfields are carved from the forest, the whole web of life is simplified. Some kinds of animals are eliminated altogether. A majority of the others still hold a place in the woods, along the edges of the fields, or in parts of the valley too wet to farm. It is there that they survive, ready for an opportunity to recover their freehold. On any walk through the less populated parts of the valley, or from any vantage point beside one of the water courses that feed into the Oyster River, these native creatures can be encountered. They give new meaning to the old landscape, and show how closely interlocked are the present, the past, and the future for all of the non-human life in the area.

Evolution

The rough-hewn landscape of northeastern America seems built to endure. Ledges of granite bulge from the soil, and except where the pioneers hauled them into lines to make stone walls, loose boulders of monumental size are randomly distributed. One enormous block, which appears to be part of the continent's very foundation, juts today from the side of Beech Hill, the highest point in the Oyster River valley. No one knows how big that piece of granite is, for only one steeply slanted face and a rounded brow are exposed. But anyone who looks carefully at the rock is soon convinced that prodigious forces were required to etch the deep parallel grooves marking its contours.

Through the sleuthing of the great Swiss naturalist Louis Agassiz less than a century ago, and the persistence of his followers, we can decipher those mighty scratches —the signature of immense glaciers which overlaid much of the continent ten or fifteen millennia before our time.

8

Whenever we take a picnic lunch to Beech Hill, we are reminded how few of the features in the landscape before our eyes antedated the Great Ice. Every plant in the valley is a descendant of an immigrant that arrived after the glaciers melted. The sand hills and gravel mounds, giant ripples below forest and orchard and pasture, are all debris left by the ice. They rest on bedrock grooved in the same pattern as the mass of granite beside us. Even the enormous boulders scattered over the valley are but trifling specks which the ice carried embedded within it. They rest where they tumbled from the melting face of the glacier, becoming obstacles too big for our forefathers to move with muscles and levers, and requiring more gunpowder to break them up than the pioneer economy could afford.

Across the stepping stones provided by the exciting discoveries of recent decades, imagination can carry us swiftly into earlier years and to a still broader view. These stones lead into a preglacial New England whose Appalachian Mountains lift peaks in a great jagged line extending northeast toward the Gulf of St. Lawrence, and in the opposite direction to outliers in Georgia. For reasons still unknown, the weather in New England a million years ago altered slightly, becoming just a few degrees cooler on the annual average. Those few degrees affected the climate upon the Appalachian peaks. The summer did not melt away as much snow as accumulated in winter. Gradually deep snowfields built up.

Looking over the Oyster River valley from the vantage point of our favorite boulder, we realize that a few extra snowflakes could not tear down the Appalachian Mountains. Each flake is so delicate and airy that its weight seems negligible. But a few inches of wet snow can load a tree branch until it breaks. All around this

9

ledge are gray birches bowed permanently by wet snows in recent winters. A few feet of snow, when added to previous accumulations, increases the pressure below until the oldest snowflakes fuse into ice pellets. If the snow cover reaches a depth of fifty feet—as it can in less than a decade—the lowest pellets fuse again, to form a solid mass of ice. When thick enough, any snowfield becomes a glacier.

On a mountain side, any glacier is likely to cut for itself a steep-walled pocket the size of an amphitheater. To do so it needs only a little meltwater when summer warms the glacier and causes it to expand. The meltwater fills the thin spaces between the glacier and the ground, freezing there and fastening the ice firmly to the rocky support. During winter, the glacier chills and contracts. Forcefully it plucks great chunks of rock from whatever surface lies below it. Year after year the process is repeated, until the glacier rests in a concave cirque of its own making.

Only a few centuries were necessary for the small glaciers in the high parts of the American Northeast to thicken, spread, and unite. As soon as any glacier is a hundred feet thick, it begins to travel. The weight of the ice liquefies the bottommost layer into a lubricant that reduces friction and lets the whole mass move down the slope. The movement produces enormous pressures on any projecting part of the ice that is caught by a rocky ledge. Such pressure may melt the projection, allowing the meltwater to run eventually into a gap in which it

Slowly the forest spreads into the shallows along the slow reaches of the river. Green flakes of duckweed spangle the surface of the quiet water. Around the edges of the swamp, arrowheads and sedges collect silt. Alders and tall trees get a root-hold.

will freeze again. Or it may break away the rocky obstruction. The rock fragments thus dislodged, like those plucked from the bottom and side walls of the cirque, become the tools of the moving ice. They groove, plane, and polish. The rounded contours of the great granite block at Beech Hill are evidence of their power. The deep furrows in its sides show in their parallel pattern that the ice grinding against them moved southeast, toward the Atlantic Ocean.

The mountainous ice once rose to an altitude through which geese and aircraft fly today. When the continental glacier reached its maximum size, half of North America lay smothered by the opaque lens which fitted the rockscape all the way south to an irregular west-east line. This, the southern limit of the Great Ice, crossed from Oregon through the Dakotas, past the present junction of the Ohio and Mississippi rivers, to Pennsylvania and Long Island. The ice topped Mount Katahdin (now 5,268 feet high) at the northern end of the Appalachian chain, and the whole Presidential Range (including Mount Washington—6,288 feet) in New Hampshire. It hid the Green Mountains of Vermont, the Catskills and the Alleghenies of New York and Pennsylvania. In some places the glacier was three miles thick, and its immense weight pressed the northern half of the continental crust deep into the earth's doughy mantle. Yet for a while the oceans could not invade the depressed land because so much of their waters had gone into the ice itself. Their basins were only partly filled.

No one knows whether the lowered level of the oceans changed the great wind-driven currents and thus the weather. It is certain, however, that the snowfall in winter came to be less than the total meltwater released by the sun to flow seaward in summer. Perhaps the tem-

"That trees are great promoters of lakes and rivers appears from a well-known fact in North America, for, since the woods and forest have been grubbed and cleared, all bodies of water are much diminished, so that some streams, that were very considerable a century ago, will not now drive a common mill."—Gilbert White, Feb. 7, 1776.

13

perature range as a whole shifted upward a few degrees. Whatever the reason, the ice melted faster than the land could recover its earlier level. Up the Hudson River valley, encroaching arms of the Atlantic Ocean connected with the Gulf of St. Lawrence, isolating the highest parts of New England as an island. Probably the whole Oyster River valley was submerged for a thousand years or more. Only gradually did the depressed land rise, providing both a destination and a bridge for plants and animals from farther south and west.

Through knowledge of weather conditions close to modern glaciers and with information from the fossil record, we can reconstruct many of the spectacular changes in the American Northeast. Even so, it is hard to realize how much the Great Ice altered living conditions over the whole continent. Between the glaciers and a line connecting the Carolinas to California, a vast tundra once spread away from the ice-hidden land. Where San Francisco, Memphis, and Baltimore now stand, herds of muskoxen and giant elephants hunted for clumps of grass among the lichens and arctic plants. Southward, in the East, a more generous rainfall and snow cover supported a dense forest of firs and spruces, which extended almost to the Gulf of Mexico. These trees, like the prairie grasses west of them, could send down roots farther than any tundra plants because they grew on soil that thawed in summer. Under tundra, by contrast, lies permafrost; only the top inch or two of mud is warmed enough in summer to let roots penetrate.

As the glaciers receded, they exposed to the summer sun the rocks they had scraped clean and polished. Spores of algae and fungi fell from the air upon the

14

surface and, under conditions of extreme adversity so close to the glacier, germinated into tiny plants that formed lichen partnerships of many kinds. When moisture was available, each fungus partner soaked it up among its meshwork of interlacing strands. When the sun beat down, the algae made use of the water in the process of photosynthesis. They manufactured foodstuffs essential to the continued life of both alga and fungus. When the water was gone or the frost returned, these pioneer plants suspended every activity that was non-essential to surviving until the rain and warmth should come again.

On the lined stone face of the great rock exposed on Beech Hill, as on so many boulders throughout the valley, lichens of a dozen kinds grow today. As we explore the trails below the trees or in the clearings, we find them taking advantage of roughnesses in granite surfaces. Yet films of water penetrate even narrower crevices. When the water freezes, it increases in volume by about ten per cent. The force of this expansion is sufficient to fracture rocks or to chip fragments from lichen-covered faces. Particles freed by frost, together with dust from the air, accumulate between each lichen and its support. They hold moisture, plant debris, and bacterial agents of decay. Such minute animals as unicells, roundworms, and wheel animalcules find here a supply of bacterial food. Although their active lives are brief, most of these creatures are like lichens in becoming dormant when cold or drought are severe. Through their contributions to the thin beginning soil beneath the lichens, they participate in a dynamic community in which the chemical ingredients for life become available for biosyntheses of countless kinds.

15

For perhaps a thousand years after the close of the Ice Ages, New England was crusted largely with lichens. Here and there, moss spores were dropped by the wind on soil of suitable thickness, and germinated. As the last remnants of the ice melted in depressions cupped by rocky rims or by glacial debris, the cold water remained as a little lake devoid of drainage. Along its margins, peat moss (Sphagnum) spread into the water. The living parts of this moss floated, buoyed up by microscopic air-filled cells. The waterlogged older parts were pressed into the lake by the weight of new branch tips above them. The products of decay from peat moss, however, were acid—a condition that slowed down decomposition. With time, the water of each isolated tarn grew dark as strong tea with these substances—and as acid as its boggy margins.

Peat moss lingers on today in many wet parts of the Oyster River valley. It fringes little bays of quiet streams and grows between the roots of black alder in shady swamps. Yet these patchy bits of spongy moss give no hint of how the valley looked during the centuries that followed the Ice Ages, for then there were few taller plants. Only little by little did even tundra vegetation move into the cold country just south of where the Great Ice still stood. Inch-high sandworts and dwarf gentians spread gradually into the thin soil between the lichens and mosses. Comparatively few kinds of flowering plants could tolerate the cold long enough to colonize the newly exposed areas. At the most measured pace imaginable, the vegetation produced the first gray-green crust covering low rocks exposed to sun and rain.

Throughout the year the stream shapes the valley. Snow and rain strengthen its flow, although sometimes a prolonged cold or dry spell mutes the song of the stream to a faint gurgle.

Bees and butterflies accompanied the flowering plants, as did eaters of seeds, insects, leaves, and meat, and their many parasites. Conspicuous among these animals were ptarmigans and pipits, lemmings and snowy owls, mosquitoes and blackflies. They moved in from warmer lands to the south and west as the second great wave of valley life. Muskoxen and caribou probably followed tundra vegetation into New England, finding enough of it to eat while they in turn served as food for blood-sucking insects and arctic wolves. Instinctively these big vegetarians chose a nomadic existence. It permitted the plants they ate to grow and regenerate despite the almost constant chill.

Muds and gravels left by the glaciers in the Oyster River valley thawed progressively all the way through to their rocky underpinnings. Seedlings of spruce and fir gained a roothold. As decade followed decade, these dark evergreens took over the territory of the tundra plants, shading them out of existence. Like broad parallel combers rolling toward shore, the arctic vegetation and the boreal trees, together with the animals they supported, followed the retreating ice. They reached the base of every mountain, slowly encircled its slopes, and rose toward the peak.

Today all of the permanent ice is gone from the Presidential Range and from Mount Katahdin. Yet the boundary between the tundra plants and the spruce-fir forest remains—close to 5,000 feet above sea level. No muskoxen, caribou, or lemmings inhabit these alpine tundras of modern New England. The ptarmigan are gone too. But the arctic butterflies continue, their caterpillars managing somehow to survive despite the annual return of the world's most violent weather.

18

Snowy owls visit New England now only when they are starved out of regions farther north. Then they fly even to lowland areas, including our Beech Hill, from which all other arctic animals and plants have vanished. Gone too are the valley's firs and spruces, except in the steep declivity of Spruce Hole. We can still visit them in this historic site, where a glacier fragment melted within a rim of gravel only 125 feet above present sea level. The peat bog at the bottom of Spruce Hole is a living relic from the tundra stage of the continent's slow recovery after the long Ice Ages.

Elsewhere in the Oyster River valley, a forest of white pines, of oaks and hickories, of hemlock and beech spreads over all the uplands. Along rivers where the sun shines in from over the water and brightens foliage near the wet soil, great willows tower above an understory of dense alders.

These and hundreds of other kinds of plants followed the dark spruce and fir forests out of the South and West. They colonized the land as rapidly as the soil was built up, giving them the living conditions they needed. But when did the deciduous trees begin to dominate the valley? It may have been no more than a thousand years ago, for the present boundary between the spruce-fir and the deciduous forests is less than a hundred miles to the north. The slow march of trees must have changed the scene in comparatively recent times. If we call thirty years a human generation, and a hundred that for a hemlock or a beech, there may have been fewer generations of these trees on New England soil since the Ice Ages than there have been of men since the Pilgrim Fathers landed.

The once-virgin forest atop Beech Hill is today represented by one giant hemlock and one old beech which is so gnarled as to be worthless for lumber. Thousands of new trees are rising. Some of them spring up in the untended right of way along the hill's southern flank. Others push into the narrow corridor of an abandoned ski jump. These former avenues are now nearly invisible from the air. They are faint indeed by comparison with a broad ribbon of unnatural grassland which is maintained across the northern slope by means of chemical sprays. For mile after mile, below the transmission towers of the power company, this ribbon undulates with contours of the land.

Three heavy cables strung from tower to tower carry energy captured by green plants in ancient forests millions of years before the Appalachian Mountains rose. Not a single kind of tree or of forest animal from those days is familiar to us except as a fossil. Every one of them became extinct—pushed out of existence by more modern descendants with the adaptability necessary for survival.

It is easy to be impressed by the increased pace of change during the last three centuries, which has occurred mainly because so many kinds of foreign animals and plants have been introduced from all over the world. As never before these compete with the native life and with each other. A few are so successful that they have become pests and weeds—chiefly on land once occupied by the forests. In this sense they are co-tenants with man, often thriving only so long as he protects them by providing food or letting the sun strike the ground. In most cases, the indigenous creatures are ready, if left alone, to crowd out the foreign kinds. Contests between species constantly attract our attention, for they de-

20

termine who survives and it is upon that outcome that evolutionary progress depends.

As we look into the forests, the meadows, and the waters of the valley, we wonder how much history will repeat itself. No one knows what disrupted the food webs and caused all of the dinosaurs to die out. It wasn't glaciation. It wasn't man, for he had not yet made his appearance. It was something far less spectacular, something fundamental that is yet to be discovered.

By getting to know more intimately the living things in territory constantly in view, we can hope to identify the features that are so vital in deciding the fate of each individual kind of creature. The natural laws that determine which contestant will survive and evolve further may govern the future of mankind as well.

Boundaries

In his charming book of essays entitled *A Sand County Almanac*, the late Aldo Leopold recommended starting out at daybreak to explore the natural world. At that hour anyone is the sole owner of as many acres as he can walk over. Both boundaries and the idea of being bounded disappear together in the dawn. For most men they reappear when the dew is gone. But in the animal world, as among plants, man's boundaries mean little.

According to the deed in the town hall, our bounds are marked by concrete posts sunk in the soil at the corners of that certain parcel of land situated at the corner of Garden Lane. At dawn and sundry other times during the day, we are more aware of owning a lunch stop on the aerial highway flown daily by black-capped chickadees, evening grosbeaks, purple finches in every stage of plumage change, goldfinches and pine siskins, hairy woodpeckers and downy woodpeckers, white-

22

breasted nuthatches for whom gravity does not seem to exist, impeccable cedar waxwings, raucous-voiced jays, and a flock of very vulgar starlings. In season this same highway knows tourists such as fox sparrows and kinglets. It serves too at ground level for baby chipmunks, on their way to conquer the New England world of stone walls.

Sometimes we think of the young chipmunks as spreading from their parental home like the concentric ripples on a quiet pond. And as with the ripples we quickly lose track of them. The one chipmunk we do know introduces a new family every year to the cantaloupe seeds and other treats set out at the end of the top step by our back door. She has a winter bedroom and a whole catacomb of storehouses for seeds under the sod of the terrace. We have no idea how often she remodels the interior, but every week or two we find the former entrance holes tightly plugged with earth and new ones opened. Occasionally she appears to forget the latest change. If someone suddenly comes up the steps on the other side of the porch, she may shriek in alarm from a flower bed and dash to where the nearest opening was the week before—only to skid into a turn at the last moment and disappear down her relocated doorway.

We recognize this particular chipmunk because of a small break in one of the dark lines bordering the pale stripe down the left side of her back. It probably marks a scar from a near-fatal episode in her past. We meet her all over our 100-by-150-foot lot, even on the roof of the house. On urgent business of her own, she scurries over the properties of our several neighbors, and sometimes crosses the roads which meet at our corner. Clearly she knows her way about on more than two acres of land. So far she has been able to reach the safety of a stone wall or a tree several jumps ahead of all the local cats which have chased her.

Until recently, the stones in our walls were loose rocks on the lot itself. By ones and twos they lay about, deeply embedded in the impoverished soil of a worn-out pasture. They afforded scant shelter to anything larger than an ant or a worm. We changed this when we laid them up along our boundaries and undertook to keep the walls mended. Our reason is unlike the familiar sentiment expressed to New England's distinguished poet Robert Frost by the man next door: "Good fences make good neighbors." We find that rock walls with good crannies encourage our smaller animal neighbors by providing them with refuges—not with boundaries.

To a garter snake or a bird or a chipmunk, a woody plant is far more meaningful as a marker than any stone wall. The true natural dividers of animal territories seem to be shrubs and trees, such as we planted in reforesting this minute fragment of the Oyster River valley. Even during colonial days, the stone walls that bisected pastures kept groups of domestic animals apart without significantly changing the area as a habitat for meadow mice and meadow larks, bobolinks and groundhogs.

The meaningful borders for the animals we see are the edges of woodland, meadow, marsh, and pond. Few marsh creatures can get a passport to set up family quarters in a pine forest. But a canopy of trees, or even a small stand of spiky evergreens, marks the landscape immediately as one for squirrels and catbirds, chickadees and woodpeckers.

The physical boundaries of our valley are unimportant to wild things. In the thin film of soil that coats the rocky glacial till, the plants grow equally well on both slopes of the low hills that rim the Oyster River basin. For animals the real boundaries match their food and shelter, and places to find mates. All of these correspond to the patterns of pond and river, forest and pasture.

Almost all the waters of the valley are connected. They provide both a living space and a highway for aquatic life. The swimmers and slow crawlers travel upstream. Everything rides the current downhill. For terrestrial creatures, the land that fingers out between the branching streams is all connected too, at least around the valley rim. By moving in darkness and avoiding the dry air of day, even animals with a skin as delicate as that of an earthworm can travel from place to place. These wayfarers go overland most frequently after a rain in spring or fall has wetted the grass and raised the humidity of the air until it is like that in the soil, or under logs, or along the edges of marshes and swamps. So many creatures travel regularly that all suitable land is kept populated with the kinds of life that can thrive there.

Only the water world fits naturally into the contours of the valley, and it alone changes more slowly than a tree can grow. Century after century, meltwater and rain trickle down the same slopes, through the same clefts in the granite, and join with other drainage into rivulets that increase in size as they approach the main course of the river. But the slopes themselves may be a home to forest creatures or to those that thrive in meadowland, according to the amount of cover provided by the trees. In our valley, the patchwork pattern of woodlands, pastures, and cultivated fields changes every year as trees rise on abandoned land and as they are burned or cut as a crop. The land animals adjust their lives to match the altered boundaries. They keep the whole valley a sampler of New England, continuous with the

25

rest of North America, and representative of similar areas all over the world.

Every spring, beginning in late February or early March, the birds divide up the countryside anew. From winter shelters in marshes along the Oyster River, the cock song sparrows move out, each to select a summer homesite. Hundreds, perhaps thousands, of these little birds fly to higher ground. One of them regularly selects the vertical green finger atop the tallest spruce in the border of trees we set inside our stone walls. From this podium he sings to the world that only one other song sparrow will be tolerated in our grove, and she must be the mother of his nestlings of the year.

How long does it take the song sparrows to agree on the relative importance of the various bushes and trees within the domain they claim? Within a few days after the cock sparrow arrives, we see that the whole grove is taboo to any other male with a streaked brown breast and a big dark spot in the middle of it. No chipping sparrow or tree sparrow has the right to inspect any of the possible nest sites within ten or fifteen feet of the one the song sparrows choose in March. No wren or robin, catbird or jay is brave enough to sit in the song sparrows' nest tree after that nest has been begun and its environs have taken on special meaning. And yet when the catbirds arrive in May, a pair is permitted to build a new nest in the spruce the song sparrow uses as a singing perch. The catbirds ignore him, although they chase away any robin or cedar waxwing that approaches their spruce—and drive every visiting catbird from the whole grove.

A few areas remain as a sort of public domain among the wild creatures that defend a territory. Just as a waterhole in Africa is a meeting place for all kinds of animals, so too in America the birds and the muskrats raising families at well-spaced intervals around ponds and along streams allow members of other species to visit the water's edge.

One small area on our lot is common property of this kind. Close to the bird bath and the several feeding trays, the one pair of resident robins accepts the presence of other residents of all sorts. Singly or in groups, these residents meet the hundreds of transients along the aerial highway, and incite no quarrels so long as the nonresidents are of other species. They rarely bicker as they perch on the twisted sumac, or the wild honeysuckle bush, or the pines hung with woodbine. Instead they fidget endlessly until it is their turn to enjoy the sunflower seeds and other foods we set out, or to get a drink. They hop along the branches for all the world like airplanes in a circling stack above a busy airport, each awaiting radio instructions from the control tower before coming in to land.

In our own bit of the Oyster River valley, we try to keep account of the boundaries the various birds defend. Beyond our walls and grove the land is equally compartmented. Countless borders important to animal life await discovery by anyone willing to take the time to watch. In the unsold parts of the original pasture, these natural subdivisions—unmarked on any map—are harder to see, for asters and mulleins are the tallest plants. Yet the markers are there, recognized by individual groundhogs and meadow larks.

It would take a lifetime to plot all of these territories. And the map completed in one week would be useless the next, for the landscape changes along with its animal life. Although it is organized so minutely on any given day, the whole pattern of boundaries is dynamic and inherently unstable. Each time a fox or an owl catches a full-grown mouse, the neighboring mice extend their territories to include the area that had previously supported the caught one. But they will not defend the addition vigorously, since its new boundaries are too far from their own homes. Eventually a healthy youngster of the same kind may fight his way into ownership of the same bit of territory. The neighbors then retire to their earlier battle lines.

The bigger the animal, the larger is the territory required to support it. This is the scientific basis for the old Chinese proverb: "Only one tiger can live on each hill." In America the fur trappers who pioneered in exploring the wilderness found the same rule applying to cougars. One of these big cats patrolled and defended an area that was roughly circular and about nine miles across. It needed all of this as a hunting ground, since a cougar's normal diet required it to kill a deer or a moose for dinner almost every other night.

Until less than three centuries ago, cougars were the biggest predators in New England. Any one of these sleek, longtailed cats might reach a body length of nine feet and a weight of two hundred pounds. The pioneers knew them as catamounts and painters, pumas, purple panthers, American lions, mountain lions, silver lions, or brown tigers. Rarely did one of these great beasts attack a man. But because they welcomed horseflesh in place of venison, they had to be eliminated.

No longer can anyone reconstruct the actual boundaries the cougars once observed in New England. From the activities of these animals in untamed wilderness farther north and west, however, we can piece together enough about their habits and requirements to visualize the recent past. It is possible to think of a mosaic of areas,

28

each of them measuring nine miles across, each the domain of one cougar, each a patchwork of forest and meadow, beaver pond and estuary border offering enough low-growing shrubs and seedling trees to nourish about seven hundred and fifty deer. Such a population of deer—about one per fifty acres—has actually been found to be close to ideal, permitting the animals to transform foliage into food for a host of different predators without endangering the reproduction of the plants.

From such a herd, about a third must have been removed annually to keep the population in balance with its habitat. The mountain lion would take one every other night, and a family of wolves roaming much the same territory would kill one deer a week as part of a broader diet. This accounts for all but sixteen of the two hundred and fifty deer to be eliminated every year, if the population were to remain stationary. Diseases could easily take those sixteen.

A mountain lion consumes seven or eight pounds of the choicest deer meat in one big meal, which will suffice for two days. The great cat then hides the remainder of each carcass under leaves, in effect abandoning it to an assortment of bobcats, foxes, and smaller meat-eaters. These animals benefit from the cougar's presence and prowess as a deer hunter, and still retain their other roles in the territory as controls on mice and squirrels, rabbits and hares, frogs and large insects.

A family of wolves, consisting of a 150-pound adult male, his 80-pound mate, and two 75-pound youngsters, might chase down one deer a week and gorge themselves twice in succession at each large kill. A first meal, averaging perhaps 20 pounds of meat apiece, would be partly disgorged into a hole dug in the ground somewhere near by, as a cache to be consumed later in the week. Wolves, unlike mountain lions, leave little to feed other denizens of the territory.

Today the hunters have destroyed the mountain lions, the wolves, and the bobcats in the Oyster River valley and all the adjacent countryside. They keep foxes scarce despite at least a doubling in the numbers of mice and deer. Four deer (or more) to each hundred-acre farm can do a surprising amount of damage to a corn field in a single night. Just one deer trying to find enough to eat at midwinter in a fifteen-acre woodlot, can destroy most of the young trees that might grow up to take the place of mature ones. A surprising number of deer still starve every year in New England, after themselves preventing the renewal of the woodlands they need for cover. Those that survive seem to know no boundaries when night has come. From hiding places they emerge after dark and spread out to feed, then dash to the nearest shelter as the light of dawn spreads across the sky.

By daybreak, when we go for our regular morning walk, the deer are safely concealed, able to rely upon their invisibility to save them from any need to run. We find their paired toeprints in the mud beside the river, large prints for parent deer and small ones for fawns. Usually the prints face the open water, where the animals have bent down their graceful heads to drink, pressing their weight on sharp forefeet into the ground where it is moist and soft. Sometimes we discover branches from which the deer have browsed a few hours earlier. The sap still glistens from the cut ends in the early light.

Occasionally, we reflect that our footprints in the mud at the edge of the river have more in common with those of the deer than the number of toes would imply. We too are oblivious to boundaries in the dark and the dusk. We are like the deer also in belonging to a species that unconsciously is reproducing itself to the limits of its food supply and living space, even though doing so means destroying its own habitat.

Deer and man developed as creatures of the forest edge, ready to hide in the shadows or emerge for food into the open places. Human forebears continued along boundaries as they emigrated, following seacoasts and traveling up waterways, never able to make a living on the open ocean or far from rivers and streams. For millennia they throve chiefly where they could carve fresh clearings for themselves from the forests they found— just as happened in New England less than four centuries ago.

No longer can there be any doubt that boundary-conscious man has benefited from his readiness to reach in any direction to secure his place in the hierarchy of living things. But his role in the dynamic balance of nature varies according to whether he gets his energy for life directly from plants as a vegetarian, or chooses the meat of animals that feed on plants. In the one role, the various carnivores and animal parasites are his friends, reducing competition for the plants he wants. In the other role, he takes his stand in the very peak of the pyramid of life and competes with the carnivores— especially the larger ones.

This variable relationship between man and his habitat has let him take the best of two worlds—the plant and the animal—but at considerable expense to both. Yet in secluded places the majority of creatures that observe boundaries are able to continue, following almost unchanged their original way of life. It is there that we can go to understand the fundamental laws of nature every living thing must follow if it is to retain its place in the world.

31

The Ponds and the River

About the time when the New World was being discovered, Leonardo da Vinci recognized that a river was
in a sense an equivalent of time. The water into which
he dipped his fingers was "the last of what has passed
and the first of that to come," just as is the momentary
present. Beside a pond in New England, Thoreau inverted this idea to proclaim: "Time is but the stream I
go a-fishing in."

From the Equator to the polar regions, on every continent and major island, fresh waters have given man
pause. Unlike an ocean, they offer him a drink as well
as food, and a better place in which to bathe. There are
no tides to toss fresh water restlessly to and fro. Instead,
fresh water follows a rhythm matching the stately sequence of the seasons.

Like millions of other people, we find contentment
while relaxing watchfully, close to the edge of fresh

32

water. Some years before we explored the Oyster River valley and made it home, we noted that when you sit by a pond or a slowly winding stream, the city's impatient tempo drains away, and from the corners of the mind thoughts come out and sun themselves. This magic works in staid New England too. We may be only as far from our responsibilities as the big rock by the pond. But our minds can ignore the rumble of diesel trucks along the state highway while our eyes and ears scan our immediate surroundings for tokens of wild native life.

Our valley offers a wide variety of ponds and streams to sit beside. Although it is only four miles across at its widest, and extends hardly any farther from the limits of tidewater to its rim, its land is dissected by more than twenty miles of stream and river. Most of these fresh waters flow south toward the noonday sun or east toward the nearby sea. In four places, behind man-made dams, they spread back into a multitude of quiet little bays where the plants and animals of lake and pond find a place to live. Elsewhere the current is more pronounced, and the amount of water passing varies from a gurgling trickle during a summer drought to a roaring torrent when first the winter's ice gives way and is hurried along by rains in early spring.

The hazards of life for plants and animals match the two extremes in fresh water: the periodic stagnancy of standing pools, and the wide variations in the force of the current through swift sections. Each of these aquatic habitats has its own community of distinctive creatures, all of them well adapted to surviving the predictable cycle of changes in their environment.

Ordinary variations in the level of a pond follow a seasonal pattern toward which particular plants are ex-

34

traordinarily tolerant. Willows and alders grow well both when their roots are in water-soaked soil and when the water level falls enough to admit air into the ground beside a pond. In many places the willows lean out gracefully, their trailing branch tips caressing the water surface, and forming a sort of arbor for aquatic animals. Alders grow more bushy, and produce a tangle through which it is hard to reach the water's edge.

At other places the ponds are fringed with a narrow marsh of cattails, which stand erect in the muddy bottom like grasses of Brobdingnagian size. Even in late summer, after low water and hot air have allowed the surface muck between the cattail roots to harden, a full-grown man feels out of place as he pushes between the cattail leaves. He feels ant-sized, for he can see no more than a few feet in any direction except straight up. No breeze reaches him, and everywhere the same kind of harsh narrow leaves bar his way.

On the water surface

From a canoe the cattails and the alder thickets appear no less dense, although many narrow channels through the marsh may be evident, as passageways that were invisible from shore. While paddling along we almost instinctively reach for the floating leaves and flowers of water lilies. Each lily pad is tethered by a long stalk to a loglike rootstock in the bottom mud. At the surface it stays all summer like an anchored ship, riding the wavelets and holding its position regardless of any slow lowering of pond level. Wet beneath and dry above, the

All the waters of the valley pour over the old dam. It was built to provide water power where the natural falls of the Oyster River separated the sweet water from the salt.

lily pad is a parasol for small fishes, a green landing field for dragonflies, a buoyant perch for frogs. At the same time it is a leaf-thin trap for sunlight, manufacturing food for growth and for storage in the rootstock down below.

Between the lily pads the jet-black whirligig beetles zig and zag singly or in flotillas. They too shed the water from their shiny backs, but are wet beneath where their flat feet paddle furiously, driving the insect along at a dizzy pace. Even the two compound eyes of a whirligig are divided, one part dry and facing into air, the other wet and keeping aware of events in the depths of the pond. These eyes are good enough to warn the insect of an approaching fish, or of an insectivorous bird diving toward the surface from above. But for making the quick changes in direction of swimming, which enable whirli-

Water lily leaves are dry above, and serve as a fine landing field for dragonflies, a resting place for frogs. Underneath, the leaves are wet and support an astonishing variety of small animals which suspend themselves from their green roof into the waters of the pond.

gigs to cavort like speedboats in a regatta without colliding with each other or with obstacles in their path, vision is not adequate. These creatures rely, instead, upon holding their antennae level with the surface film and detecting reflected wavelets of their own making. These cues are just as valuable at night.

By day the whirligigs have insect company on the surface of the ponds and slow reaches of the river: the water striders, which in Canada are called skaters and in Texas are known as Jesus bugs because they walk dry-shod upon the water. A strider's legs are long and slender. Its feet are covered with short water-repellent hairs so fine that they do not break through the surface film. The strider supports its body on its first and third pairs of legs, as though they were pontoons. With its middle pair, it rows along or even hops.

Systematically the striders investigate each leaf or petal that flutters down to the pond surface, and everything that floats up from the depths. Often the object the strider finds is a dead insect or other bit of meat into which it can thrust its sharp beak and get nourishment. Occasionally a strider creeps down into the water and sculls along slowly below the water film. With body inverted, it polices the roof of the pond from the wet side instead of the dry. Below the water film, the strider is usually a brilliant silver from air bubbles trapped among the longer of the hairs that cover its body. This covering helps in respiration, and may also hide the insect from hungry minnows looking at it from below.

In the quiet shallows

Below the lily pads and the insects at the surface are many small scavenging animals and also predatory insects, such as the strange backswimmer bugs which live

37

their whole lives upside down. Suspended like horizontal tear drops stained dark above and pale below, they wait with one long pair of rowing legs outstretched, ready to propel themselves rapidly to any meaty meal.

The backswimmers, like all the diving beetles, the water boatmen, and mosquito wrigglers, are air-breathers for whom stagnation in the pond is no problem. At intervals they come to the surface to capture a new bubble, upon which they depend as though it were an aqualung. Commonly the tip of the bubble remains visible as a silvery reflector in contact with the water. There is virtue in this position. Since each bubble begins as atmospheric air, it goes below as four parts nitrogen and one part oxygen. Soon the insect uses up the oxygen and the bubble shrinks in size. The residue of gas, now almost pure nitrogen, dissolves very slowly even in contact with the water. Oxygen, however, escapes into the bubble from solution in the water. It passes through the exposed boundary between the water and the nitrogen and gives the insect more oxygen to breathe. Only when the captive bit of nitrogen becomes too small to serve in this way do we see the swimmer return to the water surface for a new bubble.

Others of the water insects are more like fishes in that they have gills, although they rarely wave them in plain sight. So long as the pond water provides these creatures with oxygen, they need not come up from the bottom over which they creep to find their food. But when oxygen becomes scarce, as it does when stagnation sets in, they are in real difficulty.

Immature dragonflies have just such well-hidden gills. These strangely grotesque insects, which lack a distinctive name of their own and must simply be called dragonfly naiads or nymphs, inhale and exhale water from a

Although the shining steeple of the church shows how near the town is, the wild creatures of the pond continue their activities in their own way. The muskrat builds his house, and the redwings raise their families. At dusk, bullfrogs call and fireflies wink around the margins.

special chamber that opens at the rear of the body. While one of these naiads remains motionless, clinging to a water plant or standing on the bottom of a shallow pond, it resembles a little gargoyle. But the effects of its current in and out can sometimes be seen in the bending of small leaves close by. At the head end, the naiad is all attention, ready to unfold a tricky lower lip that ends in a rakelike grasping mechanism. With its prehensile lip the naiad drags hatchling fishes and smaller insects quickly to its mouth, usually after stalking them in slow motion for many minutes.

39

If hunting becomes poor, the dragonfly naiad spasmodically contracts the breathing chamber around its gills, and achieves a kind of jet propulsion. Through the water it progresses at a slow and jerky pace. Usually it holds its legs stiffly extended, as though to prove that they are not used for this unique kind of swimming.

Whenever we happen to look into a pond at the right place and time, we see a dragonfly naiad jetting through the water, perhaps right over a caddis worm that is browsing quietly on the plant debris at the bottom. The caddis worm too has gills, hidden by the tubular case that covers all but the head and parts of the first three body segments bearing the legs. Wherever it goes, the caddis worm hauls its case along, like a man holding up a barrel in lieu of clothes. The forward portions of the caterpillarlike body are the only ones equipped with armor plating; the remainder is soft. Yet when a caddis worm undulates its body within the case, it drives a current of oxygen-containing water in at the front door, over the delicate gills, and out again at the opposite end of the tube. Without its shelter, the caddis worm could not so easily replenish the water around its body and get the oxygen it needs.

When we think about the animals in a quiet pond that is becoming stagnant, we can better appreciate the great advantage a land creature gains in being surrounded by air, which is always about twenty per cent oxygen. The land animal must dare the burning sun, the drying wind, the drastic changes in temperature, all of which are unknown to aquatic life. It must exert itself merely to stand up in the unbuoyant atmosphere. But it has oxygen always available. Caddis worms and fishes and other gill breathers must manage with far less of this gas. At 68

Mallards tip up to feed on the bottom of the shallows. By staying in little groups, the birds gain in security. A few are always up for a breath of air, alertly watching their surroundings, while the others have their heads under water.

degrees Fahrenheit, the concentration of oxygen in water is less than two-thirds of one per cent.

Rarely is pond water saturated with oxygen at any temperature. Everything alive competes for the dissolved gas. So do a great many chemical compounds that oxidize readily. Throughout the day and year the supply of oxygen in the pond varies from meager amounts to almost none. After sunrise, the green plants in surface waters begin liberating a fresh supply. Yet at sunset they commence taking much of it back again for their own respiration. In late summer, waters that become choked with vegetation capture too little sunlight by day to

41

supply oxygen for nocturnal needs. Many creatures suffocate. The numbers of minnows are limited far more by depletion of oxygen and the drying up of ponds and streams than by the depredations of minks or kingfishers.

By midsummer, before the ponds grow stagnant and poor in oxygen, many of the smaller kinds of aquatic life have escaped from the difficulties to come. Hordes of insects emerge from the water to spend their adult stages in air. Dragonfly naiads become dragonflies; caddis worms transform into mothlike caddis flies. They flit about and reproduce, laying eggs near or in the water. The egg stage is often better able to tolerate both drought and the adverse chemical conditions that go with stagnancy.

A majority of the more minute creatures that stay behind while the water stagnates have another ruse for insuring new generations of their kind. As conditions for survival become difficult, they produce thick-shelled eggs or armored young that defy drought, suffocation, and even frost. Within these shells the living material is so dormant that its needs for oxygen virtually vanish for months on end.

The minnows, which rely for food almost completely upon minute creatures, cannot match this trick. As the tiny crustaceans dwindle in number, leaving only microscopic eggs as posterity, many of the minnows die of starvation. Often this change comes while oxygen is still in reasonably adequate supply.

As we poke along carefully at the edge of the ponds or paddle over the slow reaches of the river, the small crustaceans that feed the minnows rarely catch our attention no matter how numerous they are. So minute and transparent are their bodies that they can be overlooked in a glass jar full of water dipped up as a miniature

42

aquarium in which to watch a backswimmer or a caddis worm. For us to recognize them in the pond itself, we need to bring our eyes within a foot or so of the water surface. Then we may realize that the seemingly clear liquid is alive with dancing motes of life, each the size of a sand grain and actually big enough to see. So numerous are they (and suspended bits of non-living matter) in fresh water that daylight penetrates less than a fifth as far in lakes and streams as in the less populated waters of the sea.

Some of the miniature animals the minnows eat bear the names of giants—for example *Cyclops,* a pear-shaped crustacean resembling the monster of Greek myths in that it has a single blood-red eye in the middle of its forehead. *Cyclops* swims, as though at random, by twitching a pair of antennae that are longer than its body. Often the creature trails a pair of egg masses like oversize saddlebags, increasing its over-all length to perhaps an eighth of an inch.

In the world of fresh waters, *Daphnia* is not a shy maiden but a water flea that jogs endlessly up and down by waving its branched antennae, turning one way and then another as though to watch its neighbors of the same kind. Usually all of these are females, which produce brood after brood by virgin birth. The single knobby compound eye of *Daphnia* jerks into many positions under muscular control, and may be the most conspicuous part of the animal. Often *Daphnia*'s body is so transparent as to seem only a faint ghost accompanying the black eye, the C-shaped digestive tract full of opaque plant material undergoing dissolution, and the scores of reddish young that are developing pickaback within the brood chamber under the thin bivalved shell.

We would not find *Cyclops* and *Daphnia* so abundant

43

if it were not for the presence of immense numbers of microscopic drifting plants which in fresh waters are the invisible equivalent of grass on land. Although they are so small, they nourish indirectly all of the larger forms of aquatic life: the minnows, the predatory bass and pickerel, and even the kingfisher that dives for minnows. However, the more of this minute life a pond has in its sunny upper level, the darker and more stagnant are the depths by midsummer. Every creature shades the bottom ever so little. Each water flea or minnow or bass eliminates opaque wastes which settle like a solid rain of tiny particles, adding new thickness to the bottom muds. The wastes include much incompletely digested matter, which competes with living animals for the oxygen dissolved in the water.

In the dark depths

All summer, at any depth greater than about thirty feet, the bottom water is virtually isolated from the air above. Merely because the surface water is warmer and less dense, it mixes very little with deeper, cooler liquid when the wind whips oxygen into the top of the pond. Only in spring and fall, when the temperature of surface waters is about the same as that at greater depths, can the wind set the whole liquid mass of a deep pond or shallow lake into circulation, thus sending oxygen to the bottom. At other times of year, the concentration of this gas approaches zero at depths exceeding thirty feet.

Bass and pickerel, rather than trout, follow the minnows in the pond, for the trout can tolerate neither the warmth of the upper waters in summer nor the low concentration of oxygen at cooler depths. A trout, unless it can find a pool that is shaded from the sun and fed by a well-chilled stream, becomes overactive. As a result it

44

requires more oxygen and food than is available, and thus dies of suffocation or starvation or a combination of the two. Bass, which live at a slightly slower pace, are often squeezed between the warmth above and the low availability of oxygen deeper down.

Far below the bass, the minnows, the minute crustaceans, and the microscopic plants, is a muddy bottom rich in nutrient material. But where oxygen is so scarce, only a few kinds of animals can join the decay bacteria in feeding. The chief animals of the depths are blood worms, bright red larvae that eventually transform into *Chironomus* midges. Hundreds of them may writhe in a quart of mud dredged from the depths. These fly larvae swallow the muck wholesale, and so long as it is plentiful they thrive where oxygen is almost nonexistent. From their food, blood worms extract less than a fifth of the nourishment present, which is far less than would be possible if they could carry on ordinary respiration. By depending upon this inefficient chemistry of nutrition, they manage to live where other creatures fail. Sometimes the population of blood worms in the bottom sediments is so dense that the production of animal matter per square foot of muck exceeds the production of beef on the world's best pasturelands.

The production of microscopic drifting algae in the surface waters may also rival the yield of man's favorite crop plants on land. The yield of bass, however, is infinitely less than that of minute algae or of blood worms. The human species, because it overlooks such things as midge larvae and tiny crustaceans as possible food, gains from the water a really trivial amount of the nourishment present. This is equivalent, perhaps, to eating only the flesh of wolves upon the land, and rejecting all the plants and animals that supply wolves with a living, either

45

Cattails fringe the river where the current is slow. Between them, water birds find hidden channels. In seclusion the redwings build their nests, and ducks raise their families.

directly or indirectly. As the biggest predators, the muscular game fishes are the wolves of fresh water, just as the minute crustaceans might correspond to plant-eating insects and mice.

The marshy border

Often we sit where the fishermen do, looking out upon the open water of the pond and letting the spirit of the place bring us serenity. The blue sky, the white clouds, the paper birches on the far shore, the nearby bits of marsh and meadow edge are all mirrored in the tranquil surface. Then, leaving a narrow V-shaped wake, a muskrat swims across. The pair of wavelets rock all the water striders and agitate the whirligigs. The muskrat vanishes among the cattails, causing those along its track to quiver, and letting us follow its progress and imagine what it is doing.

So fond of cattail roots and young leaves are these wild rodents that they move in as soon as their favorite plants begin to grow around a pond. Since cattails provide a particularly effective trap for silt and hasten the transformation of a bay into a wet extension of the meadow, the activities of muskrats delay the change and prolong the life of the water world.

Muskrats use dead cattail leaves as building materials and for bedding. If a steep clay bank is available near by, the animal digs in it an extensive burrow and lines a bedroom or two with vegetation. Otherwise the muskrat hunts out a little island or a place so shallow that it can be converted into a spot of land by hauling up a little mud. There it constructs a low-domed lodge of mud reinforced with dead bits of cattail. The roof of a muskrat lodge is so flimsy that until it is hardened by frost, any enterprising dog or otter could break in easily. During rainstorms, in fact, the mud ceiling often sags and almost obliterates the cavity in which the muskrat crouches. Then the animal clears away the mud inside the roof and adds more mud outside, continuing until the bedroom is once more about six inches high and a foot across. Only from the entrances under water can a small predator, such as a mink, climb into the lodge. Few minks are willing to try this unless they are desperately hungry, for a healthy muskrat in its shelter will vigorously defend its life and home. An injured or sick animal is less likely to survive.

Every day the muskrat emerges from its lodge, for it

prepares no hoard of food. Often it carries a meal to a special feeding platform along the shore. Usually it is on this platform that a female muskrat bears her young—perhaps eight or nine blind, naked, helpless babies which she carries one at a time to the lodge. She may take only six or seven of her litter, and appear to forget the others. They soon die, and generally provide a meal for a turtle. With a new litter every month all summer, the mother barely has enough milk for the survivors.

Muskrats dig in the pond bottom for many kinds of roots, and favor especially the succulent tubers of water lilies. They find hibernating frogs and turtles, catch insects, and feast on clams flipped expertly from the mud. Sometimes a muskrat discovers a big fish under the ice, where partial suffocation has left it too weak to get away. When submerged foods are hard to find, the muskrat ventures out on shore and munches dry grasses, even digging for them through the snow. It attacks willow saplings as much as an inch in diameter, cutting them down and skinning off their bark as a beaver might, with skilful action of its big front teeth. By destroying willows and other woody plants that have taken root in the marsh, a muskrat slows the transformation of the wet part of the valley into forest. But eventually the plants and the accumulated silt will win out, and the place that once was a deep part of the broad river will become dry land. Then the muskrats will have to move elsewhere.

Minks are far less limited in their choice of habitat, and also have less effect on their environment. For minnows they swim in the pond; for frogs and mice and birds' nests they hunt along the bank; for crayfish and other foods the minks explore among the stones in shallow riffles. We never know where to expect a mink.

Usually one surprises us while we are intently following a kingfisher or something else. Suddenly the little black predator comes bouncing along the farther side of the river. Then all at once it slides down the bank into the water and swirls through the depths after a fish. Again, in no time at all it thrusts out its pointed head and blinks its beady brown eyes while swallowing a fish at a single gulp. Occasionally one of these sleek mammals noses near us among the vegetation on the bottom. So quickly does it move that human eyes can scarcely follow. A crayfish or a worm has little chance to get away.

It is tempting to try to make a census of the fish-eaters in our valley: the minks and otters, the kingfishers and herons, and the game fishes that become cannibals— eating young of their own kind—whenever the supply of minnows decreases significantly. The twenty-five-pound otters and the various herons are only occasional visitors to the ponds and river, but the others limit their attention to the tributaries and main course of the Oyster.

The weight of fish-eating animals is probably about equally divided among a pair of minks, some thirteen kingfishers, and a dozen medium-sized bass or pickerel. It takes about nine six-ounce kingfishers to weigh as much as one big female mink, and four more kingfishers to be equivalent to the mink's mate. To maintain these wild fishermen along the river and the valley's ponds requires a far greater weight of minnows, spaced out by snacks of mice and frogs and crayfish, worms and beetles. Each needs at least once a week to eat more than its own weight in minnows alone. The minks and game fishes require this nourishment from waters of the valley throughout the year, the kingfishers for about half as many weeks since they leave for the south in mid-

49

October and do not return before mid-April. If the average minnow weighs one ounce, the valley supplies at least four thousand of them for the pair of minks, four thousand for the game fishes, and two thousand for the birds. The ten thousand minnows amount to about 625 pounds of fish—nearly two pounds a day.

Men who study the welfare of animal populations maintain that these fishes could not continue if more than a third of the actual number were removed annually. For every minnow caught by a mink or a kingfisher or a bass, at least two fishes must escape to reproduce their own kind. If the fish-eaters of the valley eat ten thousand minnows in a year without depleting the supply, twenty thousand minnows must survive, bringing the total to thirty thousand—nearly a ton of living fish. It is thus no wonder as we watch by the water's edge that we may see a school of a hundred or so swim past every hour. Merely to feed the minks, the kingfishers, and the game fishes in the valley takes at least a hundred and eighty schools averaging this size in the Oyster River and its adjacent ponds.

Despite the apparent abundance of food, each mink lives precariously. Chronically it has trouble fending off starvation. It rapidly digests the flesh it eats, and almost as rapidly expends the energy it has gained in searching for more food. With luck and by closely heeding its keen senses, a mink goes to sleep at dusk, sleek and satiated. Upon awakening at dawn it is hungry again. A single day of poor hunting, perhaps enforced by foul weather, leaves it doubly hungry. A second such day makes it desperate, as though it knew how quickly its strength would wane. Without strength and swiftness, it cannot get another meal.

Except for man, who may regard a mink as an animal with no right to such a fine fur coat and a kingfisher chiefly as a competitor for fish, these predators have few visible enemies. Upon them, nothing preys with a regularity comparable to their predations upon fishes. This unbalanced situation rarely leads, however, to even a gradual increase in the numbers of minks and kingfishers that would cause depletion of their fish supply and a consequent crash in the predator populations. No signs of cutthroat competition are evident above the quiet river or the pond. Every active mink or kingfisher appears to find enough to eat.

The solution to this paradox lies in nature's game of Russian roulette. Every time a mink or a kingfisher bolts another fish, it risks adding to the population of parasitic worms inside its body. A few extra worms may sap its strength until it no longer has the vigor needed for catching food. The added parasites can toggle the nutritional economy to quick starvation. Man is unique in having learned to minimize this internal competition by making fire and cooking his meat—thus killing the hidden parasite—before he swallows it. Indirectly, fire is part of our secret of longevity. It helps us survive as few wild animals do, beyond attainment of reproductive prime. Without such benefits of civilization, many a mink and many a kingfisher succumbs after a single breeding season. That populations of these predators rarely increase shows how balanced is their food in bringing them both life and death.

Under the ice

In winter we still find the minks patrolling the river's edge. Once, when we judged the new ice over the pond
51

to be thick enough to walk on, we saw a small mink swimming below the transparent roof over its world. We followed at a discreet distance for about half a mile, hoping to learn what hole the predator used as a portal. The animal seemed to remember places where the ice bulged up slightly and trapped a thin bubble of air; it traveled from one air pocket to the next. Perhaps the pond turtles do the same, for some of them continue to be active, foraging among the weeds on the bottom. Until snow covers the ice, the whole water world lies there for inspection as though through the glass of a great showcase. Even the caddis worms are still dining on the thin film of microscopic plants, and they twitch their cases at the same leisurely pace as when the water is warmer. As in Charles Kingsley's *The Water Babies*: "building their houses with silk and glue" . . . toddling "about with long straws sticking out behind, getting between each other's legs, and tumbling over each other."

Until deep snow blocks out the light, the green plants under the ice continue to carry on photosynthesis during the day. The oxygen they liberate remains in solution longer than during summer, affording animals with gills a better environment for respiration; for at a few degrees above the freezing point, water dissolves almost fifty per cent more of the vital gas than would saturate it at a temperature we would find comfortable. All winter the world of the fish and the caddis worm remains at a temperature in the high thirties Fahrenheit, insulated by a few inches of frozen water from air as much as fifty degrees colder.

The Psalmist, who praised the Lord for leading him "beside the still waters," never experienced a stream stilled by a solid roof of ice. When David sang of his God, who had "set his hand also in the sea, and his right hand in the rivers," he was not thinking of a frigid

The chattering waters of the riffles hurry along too quickly to freeze. They serve as a pump, driving oxygen into the pond below its thick roof of ice and snow, enabling animals there to survive until spring.

stream such as we meet regularly in New England. In Asia Minor, hard frosts are rare and never last for months at a time.

In our valley each little cascade that remains open through a hard winter serves as a pump, pushing air beneath the ice and churning oxygen into solution. Through each rapids the water slides too quickly to be

53

chilled by those few critical degrees into immobility. Yet those seconds are enough to aerate the liquid, to the immense benefit of aquatic life farther down the stream.

The rushing waters

Within the fast water of the rapids and riffles, the water is usually well aerated. But it drags heavily against every surface and subjects the obdurate rocks to sudden battering from blocks of ice and chunks of wood floating along with the current. The water level commonly varies more where the current is swift than where it is slow. By late summer the rapids may vanish and the water shrink to a level far down among the stones. Any living things attached firmly to the rock surfaces are left exposed to air. By early spring, the river in flood may pour through at such a pace that the rocks themselves roll downstream to new positions. Only a few kinds of creatures possess the adaptations needed for existence in this hazardous niche. Most of them are insects, which match their lives to dramatic conditions on a miniature stage.

The denizens of the most dangerous sites expose themselves there for relatively brief periods—a few seconds at a time, or at the most a few weeks. Where the water curves at high speed over smooth boulders in the river, naked caddis worms set their conical nets. The fine brown threads are hardened saliva, fabricated into a mesh as regular as any fisherman would tie. There *Hydropsyche,* the net-making caddis worm, becomes a tender of nets, reaching into the pocket of mesh for any water flea or other food carried in by the current. A small *Hydropsyche* may get enough from a net a quarter of an inch across. Larger insects of this kind build bigger weirs, or even several side by side, and visit them in sequence as though they were a trapline. By staying low

54

against the stone each caddis worm is able to remain in water slowed by friction. To every roughness of the surface, it clings with claw-bearing legs that correspond to the ones a case-bearing caddis worm uses in holding firmly to its tube. These special legs are merely turned to reach the rock and anchor the back end of the body.

The *Hydropsyche* larvae build their nets to face upstream, and the current holds them tautly spread. On the same stones, the young of blackflies head in the opposite direction. By the dozen or the hundred, side by side as though shoulder to shoulder, these strangely elongate, pear-shaped creatures hold to the rock by their suckerlike back legs and extend themselves in the direction the water takes. At the point of the pear—the head end—they fan out two bristly strainers which comb from the swift water the diatoms and other microscopic plants that are invisibly suspended in it.

In the rapids of the Oyster River, as in similar places all over the world, the caddis worms and blackfly larvae must remain alert to escape the jaws of stonefly naiads which crawl stealthily about on the water-swept rocks in search of insect prey. The predatory stonefly naiads are the one-inch counterparts of mountain lions stalking wild sheep on the gale-swept shoulders of a lofty cordillera. Whereas a mountain lion that loses its footing becomes a meal for vultures and eagles, a stonefly naiad that is swept off its feet in the river is gobbled up by a fish waiting just downstream.

As the stonefly naiads work from stone to stone, the *Hydropsyche* caddis worms seem to sense danger coming and dodge away. Each one holds fast, first by the front end with its six slender armored legs, and then by the back end with its two soft muscular appendages. Crouching as though to avoid being seen (but actually

55

to stay below the swift current), the caddis worm hugs the rock. The stonefly naiad does the same, keeping its soft tufts of gills almost motionless where they project low on each side of the body.

Blackfly larvae usually wait until a stonefly naiad is upon them, perhaps until one in the group has been seized in sharp jaws and fatally hurt. Then suddenly each larva lets itself dangle an inch or more downstream on a fine silken line spun from the body tip. In the rough water the larvae bang about, and for a while it seems they will be killed anyway. Lacking any means for reeling in the tether lines, the larvae add to the silken strands in a way that suggests a mountaineering party rapelling down a steep face to a place of greater safety. No one knows how often a blackfly larva repeats this trick, moving down to another stone exposed to the current where it can cling anew. It may be repeated many times in the few weeks before the insect reaches the end of larval life, and is ready to spin an inconspicuous cocoon in which its transformation to the adult blackfly will take place.

No one misses the immature blackflies that are eaten by stonefly naiads and fishes in the swift parts of the stream, or the adults that are caught by bats and swallows and dragonflies skimming low over the water surface. The fewer blackflies the valley produces, the better we enjoy the period from mid-May until the end of June. Only at the ends of the dam, where a breeze seems to blow steadily at a rate faster than a blackfly can wing toward us, are we safe from bites outdoors.

At the dam the water splashes in a treble key upon the stones partly exposed at low tide. To these stones the smelts come from the nearby ocean to affix their sticky eggs each spring. At high tide the sound has a lower pitch, as the cascade plunges vigorously into flood-waters below. But we wonder how long the eroding cement will last, and whether the town will vote to replace the dam if it crumbles and lets the disused millpond drain. Such a change would have small effect upon the blackfly larvae, the net-building caddis worms, and the stonefly naiads in the riffles, for these all inhabit the youngest part of the Oyster River. There the count-less repetitions of spring floods have been unable to cut a deep channel through which the water can flow with-out turbulence.

If the dam goes out and the millpond with it, the cattail marsh will quickly become too dry for muskrats. A single growing season will transform the pond bottom into merely a low field, one perhaps not even flooded in spring. In a narrow channel across the middle of the new meadow, the rejuvenated river will run too swiftly for minnows to swim in and too shallowly for a kingfisher to dive into. Marine fishes, such as smelt and alewives, might be able to travel far upstream to lay their eggs—and even to eat a few blackfly larvae. The mink might catch some of the fishes from the sea, but not enough to compensate for the minnows and beetles it formerly caught in the pond during the winter. But whatever hap-pens, the river will remain the focal point of the valley, with a greater wealth of living things than anywhere near by on land.

Between a river and life itself exists a striking analogy. The great English artist and poet William Blake, born in 1757, took note of this when he wrote of "life's river." Our animals of the ponds and river spend solar energy captured originally by green plants; these alone can build the foodstuffs that sustain all animal life. Our river is raindrops and melted snowflakes—moisture lifted by the sun into sun-powered winds, and dropped on slopes within the valley's rim. Before the water goes over the dam and out to sea, the two streams of energy pass each other.

It is believed that each snowflake is an individual unlike any other either before or after. Each green plant, no matter how minute, is an individual too. It might be possible to mark components of a snowflake, and likewise the parts of a solitary green plant, with distinctive tags. Scientists do such tricks today with radioactive isotopes of chemical elements, and then follow them wherever they travel. The tagged atom in the snowflake might be traced all the way to the millpond, its origin still recognizable. The radioactive particle in the green plant might be shadowed by a persistent sleuth, into the body first of a water flea, then of a minnow, and finally of the kingfisher diving past the tagged molecule of water in the pond above the dam.

The water molecule passively takes its direction from the river, and participates in the work the river does; eroding the bed; polishing the rocks; pushing water fleas into the traps of caddis worms, and luckless minnows into the path of the kingfisher's dive. All of the energy the water gained from the sun is spent when the river drops over the dam, producing the water song we hear. The radioactive molecule in the kingfisher has a far less predictable future. It may travel to Florida, and back to the same pond. Or it may pass from the bird to other animals—to parasites or predators or scavengers— in an almost endless series as a building block of life. As we look about our valley, life is the one river for which we can see no end.

Meadows — Land in Transition

In any meadow, a groundhog can see in all directions by sitting up on its haunches. The grasses and clovers and daisies are all low enough that the sun reaches the soil between them, allowing the meadow to display a remarkable diversity of colors. In addition to the first greens of spring and browns and whites of early fall and winter, there are the special hues of summer that turn fields yellow with mustards and blue with chicory, then golden with goldenrod. Meadows change their hues more than any other part of the great patchwork of lands in our valley.

The meadow we visit most often is five minutes' walk away. Its several acres slope with gentle undulations toward the millpond from a stone wall beside a narrow rutted road. Beyond the wall is woodland, from which seedlings are forever invading the open field. Because the land faces southeast, it catches the morning sun at just about the time our neighbor strolls over the meadow each morning. In one hand he carries a strong stake, in the other the end of his cow's long tether rope. The cow plods along behind him to whatever point he chooses to stake her out for the day.

This cow cannot possibly eat all of the grasses and weeds that grow in the meadow. She has no noticeable effect upon the red clover or the white daisies, or upon the black-eyed Susans and Queen Anne's lace which bloom later in the season. By herself she would do little to keep bush spiraea and sweet fern from making the field shrubby, or to prevent tree seedlings from getting a start. But our neighbor attends to this once each summer when he cuts and dries the mixed grasses and weeds, as hay to feed his cow in winter. The haying machine keeps the woody plants from taking over.

Thoreau in 1850 wrote that he "had no idea that there was so much going on" in a meadow. So many individual plants and animals live there that each is likely to distract the eye from the next. Every day from spring until autumn, a different style of leaf or flower is unfolding, a different activity awaits discovery among the birds and insects. This is true whether the meadow is a fallow field, a stony pasture, or just the ground between the rows of trees in an orchard.

To be in the meadow at dawn on a summer day is to share a brief peace with the many animals that live there. The evidence of nighttime activities is on every hand, but the animals of the day still remain hidden where they slept. The low slanting rays from the rising sun still glint upon the slime trails of slugs and snails, and of earthworms that earlier emerged from the darkness of their burrows. The ants have not yet pushed out the sand stoppering their nests against the chill night air. The flies and bees and butterflies of daytime still cling torpidly to their sleeping perches on leaf and flower.

Each daisy is a glistening white star to any insect flying over the meadow. The flower is an invitation to a bee or butterfly, offering sweet nectar and rich pollen in return for transport of a few grains to another flower.

The warm-blooded creatures of the night have found their places of concealment. The bats, with their leathery wings folded, are in crannies where no one will notice while they finish digesting the nocturnal insects they have caught above the meadow. The groundhog sits on the mound of earth beside his burrow opening, ready to relinquish for a while all claims to the pleasant slope and the tasty weeds that grow there.

As we top the rise and descend through the open grassland, the groundhog pierces the air with a final whistle and vanishes underground. He has done this so regularly that we know where to look for him so as to see his plunge for safety. We notice other animals which are partly hidden, each in a favorite vantage site overlooking the meadow—the place from which danger is most likely to come. On previous mornings we have

61

come closer than they could tolerate, and seen them dash to alternative places of concealment.

The cottontail rabbit raises its long ears and sniffs the air for new odors. It has been snoozing fitfully below a tangle of blackberry bushes along the high edge of the meadow ever since the sky brightened before dawn. By then its stomach was full, for the rabbit during darkness trimmed most of the clover plants on nearly a quarter of an acre without attracting the attention of a fox or vigilant owl.

A doe deer and her half-grown twin fawns lift their ears and noses in their lookout among the bushes at a break in the stone wall. Without making any sound or movement that might betray their positions, each of these animals watches intently. Their stomachs are full too, with a salad-like sampling of many different plants picked daintily in the night as the trio browsed their way from the edge of the woodland to the river and back. Unless we remain motionless for many minutes—longer than their attention span—the doe and her fawns cease even to chew their cuds.

The birds of the meadow appear less concerned—so long as no one goes near their nests. Meadow larks, which are really not larks but relatives of the blackbirds with yellow, brown and white feathers and a black V-shaped bib, continue their loud whistling. Sometimes a flock rises out of the grass, almost like a covey of quail. Vigorously the meadow larks beat their wings, then glide with their white outer tail feathers conspicuously displayed. Every one of them is a male bird. Often a single individual flies up to the top of a post or to a branch of a tree along the edge of the meadow, there to whistle *WHEEyou*. Soon he may glide down to where his mate is hidden in a grass nest roofed over by living grasses. He helps her incubate the brown- and purple-spotted eggs. But we marvel that the pair ever succeed in raising a family in a place that is so likely to be stepped on by the cow or raided by some predator. Snakes by day, and foxes and skunks by night, spend a great deal of effort in searching for birds' nests upon the ground.

Near a wild cherry tree in a narrow gully that is too rough to mow, the bobolinks have a very similar nest. But the male bird rarely comes to it until the eggs have hatched and his brood need more insects than his mate can bring. In the meantime he hovers within sight of the nest, and performs a sort of aerial strutting with his beating wings carrying him forward very slowly, like a miniature helicopter. All the while he sings loudly his bright bubbling song, and shows off his white markings on wings and rump, and the golden feathers behind his head and neck.

The female bobolink, like the female meadow lark and the female redwing blackbird, resembles a big brown sparrow streaked above and below in patterns that blend wonderfully well with the meadow plants. Quite often a male redwing joins the male meadow larks and bobolinks early in the morning. He walks among them, hunting for slow-moving insects, eating an occasional seed, but never flaunting his fine red-and-gold epaulets before the other birds. Only when he starts back toward the marshy corner of the meadow is he likely to circle slowly, raising his distinctive colors in full display during a short glide, and delight us with his vocal signature: *gurgulƐƐƐ!* His mate is incubating eggs by herself among the reeds, where the pair have a compact cup of plant fibers lined with fuzz from cattails.

63

The grass and weeds are alive with insect food for birds. But to enter the insect world of Lilliput, the best way is to lie prone. When one's chin rests on the earth and one's eyes are only a few inches above the ground, each daisy towers skyward. Clovers and grasses form the horizon. A granite boulder is a mountain. This is the part of our valley that is hottest by day, coldest at night. The vegetation blocks air movement among the grass-roots, yet admits the full heat of the sun and does little to keep heat from radiating away in darkness toward the stars.

Ants forage endlessly over the baked soil, up and down each plant. Some of them discover plant lice sucking sap under the leaves or from a growing stem. The ants take turns stroking the plant lice with their antennae, inducing the sucking bugs to exude droplets of sweet honeydew. Both kinds of insects ignore the ladybird beetles that are systematically devouring plant lice, and destroying the sources of the honeydew.

On a daisy stem, a spittle insect shoves itself out of its self-whipped froth, ready to shed its skin a final time to acquire wings as a full-grown leafhopper. An inch-worm, on its way to the soil to pupate after feeding on the daisy leaves, seeks to find a route around the mass of spittle. A cutworm climbing down another weed is twisting this way and that, trying to avoid a persistent fly. But the fly succeeds in stabbing a few eggs into the cutworm's skin. From those eggs the grubs of the fly will enter the caterpillar's body and take the food stored by the victim, using it for the development of more parasitic flies. All of these insects are snapped up by the meadow larks, the bobolinks, and the redwing blackbirds.

Hundreds of spiders lie in wait for the insects, and are so intent upon their hunting that the nearness of a human observer does not disturb them. Black-and-white jumping spiders leap upon their prey from distances as great as eight or ten inches. As they whisk through the air between the lowly plants of the meadow jungle to pounce on a bug or a fly, the jumping spiders pay out behind themselves a fine safety line of silk. Along it they can always return to the place from which they sprang. The tan-and-black wolf spiders, which run along the ground, leave no silken trail as they travel from one ambush to the next. They circuit the broad carpets of gray cobwebs laid out by grass spiders, which hide near one edge in a funnel-shaped cave of silk. They avoid also the places where doily spiders tend their horizontally suspended nets.

In the early morning, no one needs to stoop to see the webs the doily spiders spun in the grass during the night, as though setting the table for a banquet. Dew spangles every one of them. It hangs too in sparkling globules upon the orb webs hung vertically at a higher level in the low vegetation. Each orb-weaver lurks in a corner of her web until a flying insect blunders into the spiral of sticky strands that loop between the strong radiating lines.

Even the daisies are booby-trapped. Facing the center of many a flower is a milk-white crab spider with yellow legs, waiting to seize a small bee or a butterfly. So well do the crab spiders match the glistening petals of the marguerites that birds seldom discover them. And by the time the white daisies have withered for the year, the same spiders turn butter-yellow all over and proceed to benefit from camouflage in the flowers of black-eyed Susans.

65

A few of the lesser creatures in the meadow wear distinctive color patterns. These may help a bird learn that a disagreeable flavor matches the warning marks. The hairless caterpillars of the monarch butterfly, which feed on milkweeds, wear gay stripes of white, black, and yellow encircling the body, making them easy to see. Seldom do we pass one of these insects without stopping to marvel at its way of life and the strange habits that correspond. No other insect in the valley is so unbird-like in appearance, yet eventually so birdlike in behavior.

The monarch caterpillars reach their full length—about two inches—after the milkweed flowers wither, at a time when slender green pods barely an inch long are develop-ing in their place. Soon the pods will be three times their present length and plumpness. Their pale dusty-green walls will crack open to release the satin-tufted seeds. Now, however, the pods are less noticeable than the caterpillar that is holding itself underneath the stalk of one pod. Here from glands beside its jaws, the caterpillar is spinning a button of gray silk. Its task completed, it turns about and securely works its rearmost legs into the silk, then lets itself hang head downward.

Within a few hours the striped skin along the cater-pillar's back begins to split lengthwise. Inside the skin the creature works its body and gradually exposes a strange cylindrical chrysalis of pale green, embossed with a few tiny gold dots. Quickly the old skin slips up and becomes loosely bunched around the tapering abdomen. But the chrysalis pinches hold of the skin and clings firmly to it while freeing the abdominal tip. Wriggling like a contortionist, the chrysalis reaches up-ward with the black tip of its body and works the fine hooks there firmly into the button of silk. At the same

66

time, it wipes the old skin out of the silk, breaking the empty legs away from the fibers. Then, with a good grip on its world, the chrysalis releases the useless skin completely and straightens out. The shriveled skin tumbles to the ground like a discarded bathing suit.

A caterpillar needs only a few minutes to transform into a chrysalis. But the butterfly will not emerge until ten or eleven days later. By then the handsome brick-red color of the butterfly's wings shows through the clear wall of the chrysalis. The black markings and white dots on the developing insect are all distinct. When the dramatic moment arrives, a slight crack opens in the clear covering, along one of the visible lines of weakness. Inside the insect wriggles. The gap widens and lengthens. Suddenly something gives way, and the whole insect pulls itself out—legs, feelers, the soft body, and quickly the scale-clad wings, each the size of a crumpled postage stamp. Clinging below the empty chrysalis, the butterfly pumps vigorously with its abdomen, driving blood into the thin spaces within its wings. Rapidly these expand and take their adult form. As they dry they harden. Muscles and nerves that had no role during the caterpillar and chrysalis stages are ready to control those wings in vigorous flapping flight. Eyes and antennae developed during the transformation will guide the insect on its way.

The way of a monarch for the winter is the way of the migratory bird. Just such a butterfly, made recognizable by a numbered paper tag near Toronto, Canada, on September 18, 1957, was found alive on January 25, 1958 in San Luis Potosi, Mexico—some 1,870 miles distant—where it was spending the winter. Typically all the autumn survivors among milkweed butterflies

a

b

c

The change from a creeping, leaf-eating caterpillar on milkweed to a far-flying butterfly on
black-and-orange wings is one of the miracles of
the meadow. Once fully grown, the caterpillar
suspends itself from a button of silk and sheds
its skin to expose the pale green chrysalis (a and
b). After a few weeks, the colors of the adult
insect show through the transparent chrysalis (c).

d

e

When time for emergence arrives, the chrysalis bursts open and the butterfly climbs out (d) to spread its wings (e) and harden its body. The insect may fly from Maine to Florida and back before laying eggs on another milkweed plant.

hatched in Canada and the northern United States, including the Oyster River valley, migrate south. After spending the winter beyond the reach of hard frost, the fertile female butterflies wing their way back in spring, to lay eggs on new milkweeds and insure further generations in the North.

As we watch a monarch drying its wings, clinging upside down below a milkweed pod, it is tempting to wonder whether the insect or the green plant has the more complicated built-in instructions for producing a new generation. With luck, one chrysalis releases one butterfly, capable of guiding its muscular flight southwest and northeast for more than three thousand miles at the proper seasons. At the end of its long trip the insect may still be able to lay the eggs from which four hundred caterpillars will emerge, each one by itself on the proper kind of plant. Usually each milkweed releases about four hundred seeds, each capable of riding its parachute wherever the wind carries it, and of germinating in the moist soil next spring. Perhaps one seedling and one caterpillar will mature and reproduce itself from each of the four hundred that started out. That both are successful ways of life is proved by their survival through millions of years. Yet their differences are greater than might be guessed from discovering a green chrysalis hung below a green milkweed pod.

From a higher vantage point

Many of these dramas in miniature vanish with altered perspective when we rise up to walk elsewhere in the meadow. But once a person realizes how many creatures rely for food upon insects among the knee-high weeds, the discovery of the larger insect-eaters becomes a game. Some of them perch in plain sight, often with evidence of

70

their work close by. On a leaf beside the road at the forest edge of the meadow a one-inch robber fly may be sucking the juice from a honeybee. On the ground below are the empty bodies of a dozen other bees, giving some idea of how many the fly destroys in a single day.

Despite their predatory habits, robber flies are often unsuspicious, and let us come close to watch. As soon as the emptied body of the bee has been dropped among the others, the fly starts after a new victim. Rarely does a bee that is busy in a flower have a chance to use its sting, for the fly pounces suddenly and grasps its prey with all six hairy legs at once. Into the bee's back it drives a sharp beak. Almost at once the bee's struggles cease, and the fly carries its victim to the perching site to enjoy the meal.

If we cross the narrow road and lean against the stone wall under the overhanging trees, we can still keep the robber fly in view, but we are more likely to discover that the fly is not the end of the food chain in the meadow. A stately kingbird flicks his white-banded tail, drops abruptly from his place on a tree branch, snaps up the fly, and returns to his lookout point. Kingbirds eat some honeybees too, but seem able to identify the stingless drones and to choose them, perhaps by noting some difference in behavior. Robber flies, by contrast, catch mostly the worker bees whose labors are so vital to the colony.

The worker honeybees are already visiting the freshly opened flowers early in the morning, before the moisture from the nighttime mists has evaporated among the lowly plants. After a day of rain, even more of them are active. Other insects may be slightly tardier. But while the humidity is high in the meadow, the toads are on the alert. Beside the path we often find one facing

71

an open dandelion just an inch away. It stares "straight ahead after the fashion of the Buddha," just as Joseph Wood Krutch has described so well. The motionless toad studies each insect visiting the dandelion, and decides on the basis of personal experience whether or not to seize it.

Experience teaches toads to avoid all insects that closely resemble those with stings. Some harmless flies, which have the shape and color patterns of bees and wasps, mimic them so well that they escape too. But when a different insect comes along, the toad flicks out its sticky tongue, faster than human eyes can follow. Expertly it flips the victim into its capacious stomach. With luck, the toad gets a robber fly that is busy subduing a bee on the flower. Both insects disappear together into the toad's wide mouth, the fly still clinging to its prey.

As the sun dries the air and the moisture in the topsoil evaporates or sinks down among the roots of plants, the toads dig themselves backward into the ground. But along the low side of the meadow, where some of the water reappears at the surface in seeping springs, the grasses grow more lushly and the humidity does not vary so much. There squat the frogs, waiting toadlike for small insects to pass within tongue's reach. Their wet skins are poorly fitted for exposure to dry air, and when drought threatens, it is to the river or the muddy bottom of a pond that the frogs retire to await a better day.

So long as "daisies pied and violets blue . . . do paint the meadow with delight," one might well long "to be a frog, my lads, and live aloof from care." But Shakespeare and Theocritus may not have considered the many dangers a frog faces even at the most auspicious time of year. Young frogs (and toads too) may lose their lives by day if a crow or a killdeer alights near them, and by night if a skunk or a fox comes through the grass. Even after reaching full size, they are preyed upon by big snakes that patrol narrow strips of territory all the way from the stone wall to the river. Ambrose Bierce in his *Devil's Dictionary* pointed to the place of these familiar animals by using a simple food chain in his definition of the word *edible*: "Good to eat, and wholesome to digest, as a worm to a toad, a toad to a snake, a snake to a pig, a pig to a man, and a man to a worm."

In our meadow, the snakes are fairly safe during the day since no pigs are loose there. Once we watched a large garter snake, striped conspicuously in black and gold, stretched on the path that leads downslope from the narrow road. In its mouth it held a big toad, which was puffing out its body with air in what looked like an effort to be impossibly huge. For hours the snake worked its unhinged jaws, first one side and then the other, to get the toad turned and heading inward. Then, little by little, the snake stretched its mouth around its prey. The toad became merely an egg-shaped swelling partway back in the serpent's streamlined body.

For the snake, the only time limit on this process was imposed by daylight. Unless the reptile finished its meal and retired to the safety of its hideaway in the stone wall at the upper border of the meadow, a fox was likely to kill and eat it at night. Or the same fate might befall it in the jaws of a raccoon, an opossum, or a skunk. For the fox, a snake for dinner is better than going hungry after the cottontail rabbit escapes into the blackberry tangle. For the raccoon, a snake with a half-digested toad inside is an easier victim than the slippery frogs in the grass in the wet corner of the meadow. For an opossum or a

73

skunk, any snake—with or without a toad—is just another opportunity to add variety to a mixed diet.

To see these larger animals in the meadow, it is best to watch at dusk or in the light of a full moon. Human noses gain few cues at any time of year from the general scent of earth and low plants. But ears can delight in the spring calls of frogs and toads, the love song of the woodcock spiraling above the marshy end of the big field, or the summer cries of killdeers and the chirps of crickets. In the long twilight, eyes can detect the nighthawks and bats against the sky. A meadow interposes few obstacles to the effectiveness of the senses.

A dry buzzing in the dark grass may draw attention to a May beetle that is about to take off on its first flight. For as much as a year the insect has been growing as a C-shaped white grub underground, feeding on the roots of grasses and weeds. Somehow it has been overlooked by the moles that burrow in the meadow in search of insects and earthworms. Now the mature beetle is ready to take its chances while searching for a mate. Only a few of its kind will succeed. The others become food for insect-eating animals that would be less efficient if they ate the plant materials that nourished the white-grub stage of the beetle. Many a May beetle is seized by a killdeer and shared with her chicks. The fox may catch both the mole that missed the white grubs, and the killdeer chicks that ate the matured May beetle. The food relations in the meadow form a great web with many alternative links. Thereby the plant and animal community gains in continuity, in stability, with few explosive increases in the numbers of individual kinds.

By day the predators rarely show themselves in the meadow. Even when a sparrow hawk pays a visit, it

74

does so inconspicuously. From our vantage point by the stone wall, where wild creatures are less likely to notice us and be alarmed, we scan the downslope toward the river. Under an occasional breeze the weeds sway gently, but the scene recalls the "pleasing land of drowsy head" that the Scottish poet James Thomson immortalized two centuries ago. Suddenly we are aware that a sparrow hawk is hovering above the grass, intent on a grasshopper or a meadow mouse.

Whenever possible we follow the little hawk with our binoculars, to see what prize it clutches in its sharp talons as it rises after making a strike. Seldom does it miss. Rarely is its prey a bird. Insects and big spiders comprise more than half of the sparrow hawk's diet, and of the remainder, mice outnumber sparrows about two to one. Often this hawk seems to catch small birds only when they are too sick and listless to escape. Perhaps the name sparrow hawk is a misnomer. It would be better to call it a grasshopper hawk or a kestrel—the name of its nearest kin and counterpart in the Old World.

The prolific meadow mice

Except for the meadow mice the hawk carries off, we rarely see these rodents until haying time. Then, if the farmer cuts his hay, rakes it into windrows, and leaves it overnight, we can find plenty of meadow mice under its shelter. There is no need to wonder how the sparrow hawk finds enough mice from early spring until late fall. Meadow mice multiply almost as fast as an electronic computer. The hawks (and the owls and foxes and neighborhood cats) have to work hard to keep up!

Meadow mice in the Oyster River valley play the same role as lemmings do on the arctic tundras. Efficiently they transform plant materials into meat. Each short-legged, full-bodied meadow mouse grows to be about six inches long. To do so it eats about twenty-three pounds of hay a year, often knocking down and wasting an equal amount in the process. Although a meadow mouse family is small, with only four to eight in each litter, and although the babies are not weaned until they are nearly two weeks old, the female offspring are usually mothers in their own right eight weeks after being born. Almost immediately they begin another family.

Between early March and late autumn, a female no more than normally promiscuous for a meadow mouse can produce a dozen litters. If no casualties occurred, one pair of young meadow mice on March first would have more than two hundred and thirty-five *thousand* descendants, all alive before winter came—and be ready to resume reproduction the following spring. Only consistently high mortality prevents a plague of meadow mice. Even then, as many as twelve thousand to the acre (one mouse to each four square feet) sometimes mature, accompanied by almost complete destruction of the meadow plants.

After winter snows arrive, the meadow mice continue to be active. Mostly they tunnel under the white blanket, finding food among the flattened weeds. Sometimes, however, they emerge and scamper over the surface. This happens most often during darkness, when they seem unable to distinguish between the limitless cavern of night above the snow and the dark spaces below it. Under the stars, foxes and weasels and owls all pounce upon the running mice, gradually reducing the number that survive until spring.

No matter how snowy the winter, the predators and

76

the mice are rarely kept separate for long. After each new snowstorm, passable avenues open between the surface and the soil. From the hilltop and all exposed places, the winds whip away the snow. From slopes tilted toward the south, the sun evaporates the surface layers, particularly around each dry stem that remains vertical from the weeds of the previous year. Small patches of bare ground keep spreading, only to be covered again temporarily by another snowfall.

In one or two winters of every decade, the mice in the meadow meet a new predator. From the arctic tundras, a great many snowy owls move south. Perhaps the supply of lemmings in the Far North is unseasonably small. In the Oyster River valley the stately white owls take up solitary stations on the snow for daytime hunting. They appear to squint, by raising the feathers around their eyes until only a slanting slit remains to see through. Toward dusk, each owl relaxes again. Its feathers settle back, exposing the whole circles of its big golden eyes.

For the arctic owl, the snow provides a natural background, one against which the bird disappears at any time of day. Often, however, an owl settles in the top of an apple tree overlooking the meadow, and peers from this vantage point over the substitute tundra. Any other owl perched so conspicuously would soon attract a mob of crows. But not the snowy! Any crow that pauses for a close look beats a hasty retreat as soon as the owl spreads its great white wings—as much as sixty-six inches from tip to tip—and lunges at its black tormentor. Smart crows escape. Small birds seldom come close, and the snowy owl seems unaware of them. Domestic pigeons too appear to mean nothing to this regal visitor from the Far North. But any herring gull that settles on the meadow near a mousing owl seldom gets away. Perhaps this is because gulls in the Arctic menace the eggs and nestlings of owls breeding there, as they do also those of many waterfowl.

When the snows go, the great white birds vanish too. The meadow becomes a rough brown slate upon which animals scrawl their individual trails. Rarely can we follow a track for any distance, but fine details give a better chance to recognize its maker. To be sure of a creature's identity, it is better to wait until an animal walks or creeps in plain view across a muddy place. Then an inspection of the spoor allows new insight into the scute prints of a garter snake, or the six-legged scratchings of a ground beetle. The beetle hunts for caterpillars or earthworms exposed by day. The snake is ready to seize either of these, or the beetle while it is intent on capturing some prey.

Old age in a young meadow

In any season the meadow seems as unruffled as the surface of the pond. The hum of bees in clover, the occasional lowing of the cow, the songs of the meadow birds, the chirping of crickets and grasshoppers are all peaceful sounds. Yet among the lowly plants so many animals depend on eating other animals that it seems unlikely for any of them to survive into old age. Probably the life of a ground beetle or a meadow mouse is seldom as long as a year. A sparrow-sized bird may spend several summers in the meadow before accident or disease overtakes it. But creatures that last longer than an annual plant usually have some secret of longevity.

Our neighbor the garter snake is doing well. Six years ago we harmlessly clipped the corner of one scale beneath the serpent's tail, to give it a distinctive mark. Every

78

summer since then we have found the snake at least once, always in the same territory: a world about twenty-five feet wide and perhaps two hundred and eighty in length. Captive snakes of this size have survived almost as long as a pet dog—about twenty-five years. In the wild they are less likely to continue eluding foxes or large hawks for so long.

The Methuselahs among insects come regularly into the meadow from the forest edge, unwillingly and often still protesting their unreadiness to die. They are the seventeen-year cicadas, oldest of the valley's six-legged creatures. At midsummer, the males in the tree tops

The tiny white flowers of wild carrot are grouped in flat-topped clusters which have earned the romantic name of "Queen Anne's lace." The cultivated carrot was derived from this pasture weed of Asia, which is now a widespread and favorite field flower.

drum out their whining sirenlike calls. Mated females knife their ovipositor blades lengthwise into the bark of slender branches to insert a few eggs, from which hatchlings will drop lightly to the soil far below. Sucking the sap from roots, the young cicadas grow in underground tunnels for seventeen years before emerging into the air. Then each crawls to the trunk of the nearest tree, where it clings to the bark while splitting its skin to emerge as a winged adult.

After a cicada has flown to the tree tops, it rests inconspicuously. From the gravel road at the crest of the meadow, we are likely to see it again through binoculars only when it is about to be pounced upon by a big solitary wasp that hovers like a hummingbird among the branches. The wasp in the crown of the woodlands is the cicada-killer, whose body is lighter and more slender than those of the squat drummers and their mates. The wingspan of the wasp is slightly less than the three-inch spread of a cicada.

When the hunting wasp discovers a cicada clinging to the tree, she dives in for the attack. A male cicada breaks off suddenly in mid-song, and then buzzes a high-pitched brief whine as the wasp's sting delivers its first stab of venom. The cicada launches itself into the air, but the wasp is ready for this too. With long golden legs she seizes the doomed insect and hugs it to her. Beating her amber-colored wings furiously to support both herself and her prey, she turns in flight and heads for the open meadow.

The wasp descends on a long power glide, and we run to where she touches down, still with the cicada firmly held. Almost at once she turns it over, and after expertly exploring it with her body tip, stings again at a point between the victim's legs from which her poison

To the meadow the cicada-killer wasp brings her heavy prey.
Over the soil she hauls her trophy to a burrow she has dug.

will quickly reach its nervous system and quiet its con-
vulsive movements. Rarely does the wasp hesitate for a
moment more. Straddling her prize, she lifts it and starts
walking in the direction of a burrow she dug in the soil
of the meadow before starting out on her hunting trip.
Occasionally the wasp must turn about to pull the cicada
through clumps of grass and obstructing stems. But
promptly she resumes her course. For half an hour or
more she struggles to get the heavy insect to her burrow,
where she shoves and pulls it underground.

On the buried cicada, which is merely tranquilized
with venom, the wasp lays a single egg. Between the
lancets of her sting she extrudes the egg with exquisite
care and pushes it gently into a position of security atop
the prey. After she has closed the doorway to the subterranean cell, a maggot will hatch from the egg and
begin feeding on the living food she has supplied. One
cicada will suffice. The wasp selects only victims con-

siderably larger than herself, and consequently needs to provide just one for each of her larvae. Almost at once the wasp begins digging a new chamber, to be stocked with another cicada—one still to be found—in which to lodge her next egg. By spacing her offspring several feet apart in the field, she makes it less likely that a mole burrowing through the soil will find and destroy them all.

The cicada-killer links the meadow in which she and her mate matured with the forest where she finds her prey. She supplies her young in the field with cicadas from the woodland—without, however, seriously interfering with the population of the cicadas, since many of them have already mated and laid eggs before they are caught. Yet the young of the wasp, when they emerge with the same complex instincts, will have no opportunity to catch the young of the identical cicadas. When the new generation of wasps appears, the cicada young underground are still very immature—only one year along on their seventeen-year road to maturity. The new wasps prey instead on a different brood of cicadas, linking their own one-year cycle to a different population of their long-lived prey. Seventeen generations of wasps will repeat this amazing feat before any particular brood of cicadas comes up to the open air again.

While for seventeen years a new generation of cicadas is maturing in the soil, plenty can happen to the meadows. A meadow, if nothing is done to maintain it, changes faster than a pond or a woodland. If the woody shrubs that invade it are left alone for a few seasons, they transform the open meadow into a dense thicket. Wherever the rain and snow come regularly enough to support plants of woody kinds, open fields are not actually a permanent part of the landscape. Instead they are places for opportunists, for living things that are well adapted to raising new generations quickly and abundantly, then moving elsewhere. They are frontiers in which special kinds of plants and animals can take advantage of the chance to benefit from solar energy falling where temporarily the trees no longer stand and shade the ground.

With age a meadow changes gradually. In the wet corner, where marsh marigolds bloom luxuriantly in the trickle of water from seeping springs, pussy willows begin to spread. At first they interfere little with the prodigious leaping of slick-skinned grass frogs, and the bittern still "bumbleth in the mire" just as his European cousin did in Chaucer's day. In the open shade near the willows, the brilliant cardinal flower flashes above beds of blue forget-me-nots. Freckled orange flowers of jewelweed open later in the season, then fade and produce ripe capsules. We tap them to see the seeds ejected explosively—a habit that has earned the plant its other name of "touch-me-not." Yet all of these flowers may soon be shaded out by a dense stand of alders that rises above the willows. Through the interlacing crooked branches, warblers dart for a while each spring. But only a few birds, such as the woodcock, remain to nest when the alder leaves spread out. The nesting birds are seldom those of meadow land.

For a few years, wherever the open field in winter holds snow in saucer-shaped irregularities, the grasses and weeds continue to grow well. Slowly, however, slender arching stems of blackberry and bramble rise up as though they had been planted. At random, mice and birds have dropped the indigestible seeds from which they grow. The thorny briars continue to extend higher. They bend over, multiply, leaf out, and compete for

83

A few bluebirds continue to nest in the valley, usually near the apple orchards and along the edges of the meadows. From this dead cherry tree four little bluebirds were added to the population of the valley from this one brood.

sunlight with the grasses and lower weeds. Tangles of tough stems provide wonderful hiding places for cottontail rabbits. But they also eventually shade out the plants that the rabbits like to eat.

Even on the knolls, from which the winter winds blow away the snow, taller and stiffer plants start growing during the spring rains. The nutlets of sweet fern sprout, and the delicate heart-shaped beginnings of true ferns such as bracken take hold. They thrive where the meadow soil becomes driest during the summer months. In just a few years these plants rise two or three feet

84

above the soil and thus doom the grasses. Just as gradually the food for meadow animals diminishes. The leaves of sweet fern are wonderfully fragrant when crushed, but few creatures eat them. Almost no animal finds bracken fronds edible after they unroll from the springtime succulence of the fiddlehead stage. Between the upright stalks a groundhog or a pheasant can run easily and not be seen by any hawk or owl. But as the meadow changes, most of the meadow creatures move to open land elsewhere. Even the ants that live on honeydew and grass seeds abandon their nests and depart.

A herd of cows or a flock of sheep does much to slow the aging process in a meadow. Yet these animals show little liking for the seedlings of staghorn sumac, of red cedar, or of gray birch when these appear. Long before one brood of immature cicadas completes its growth, the pioneer trees of pastureland can grow twice as high as a man's head. Each spring they close off the winter vistas in a mist of fresh green foliage. Each summer they provide browse for deer, and hiding places for more fawns. Each fall the old meadow is ablaze with sumac leaves in wine reds and tawny browns. With the constant green of cedars, the gold of birch contrasts sharply. Each winter the waxwings come for the sumac fruits, and juncos work over the catkins that the birches have prepared for the coming spring. Yet these trees, the invaders of the meadow, rarely have a chance to reproduce themselves on the same soil. They shade out the lowly plants, but by the same token they shade their own seedlings. They are replaced gradually by pine and sugar maple, hemlock and beech, whose seedlings thrive in shade. It is the shade-loving trees that finally inherit the meadow—and the whole of the valley land.

The Valley's Woodlands

In the woods, life is on a far grander scale than anywhere else on land. Neither the water world nor the meadow has plants to compare in height or bulk or wealth of leaves with the tall trees. No animal inhabiting the ponds and streams, the fields and orchards, is equivalent to the two hundred-pound bear and deer that find food and shelter along the forest edge. By their size and variety these living things show what the soil and climate can support if given time. But for a forest, time is measured in centuries, if not in thousands of years.

In our valley, the tree that foresters regard as the oldest is a white pine about fifty-two inches in diameter at chest height, whose age they estimate at two hundred and fifty years. Fondly known as the Paul Bunyan pine, it is a deformed giant only a hundred and twenty feet tall. Had some misfortune, perhaps an attack by a caterpillar of the Nantucket pine moth, not destroyed its leader about a century ago, the tree might have grown straight and, at its present age, have attained a height of perhaps forty-five feet more. Still this venerable living monument is only three-quarters grown. It has escaped the woodsmen for so long, and acquired such a reputation, that it may be let survive another eighty or a hundred years. It may even demonstrate how long a white pine can live.

Around the Paul Bunyan tree are many younger, slimmer, more shapely pines. They tower almost as high above the forest floor, and may well be the giant's offspring. Close together in its shade they grew and followed the tradition of white pines by dropping off every whorl of side branches all the way to their lofty crowns. Now they stand clean-lined and straight, clad only in flat flaky bark that is sculptured with shallow lengthwise channels.

Among the white pines and throughout the valley's woodlands, hardwood trees reach the girth and height of the Paul Bunyan pine in about three centuries. Most of the hardwoods are sugar maples, shagbark hickories, white ash, red oak, or beech. To the casual observer, walking between their trunks and unable to reach any leafing branch, all except the hickories appear similar. But no one can overlook the distinctive shagbark, which scales off in long irregular pieces all the way up the bole.

Still younger trees vie with lower-growing kinds in forming an understory below the tops of the giants. Some of them are slender canoe birches, whose snow-white bark in paper-thin sheets is marked by narrow breathing slots crosswise of the trunk. Even when old and flecked with black, the birches brighten the colonnades between the tall trees. Whenever wind tosses their leaves high above the ground, slivers of sunshine may slip through to the lowest level of plants, dappling their foliage with momentary spots of light. Only where the understory is the dense tier formed by the branches of evergreen hemlock is the soil of the forest dark at midday. Few seedlings can capture enough solar energy to grow under the soft needles of a big hemlock. But elsewhere the forests of the valley are carpeted with green.

Nights are longer and days shorter in the forests than elsewhere on land in the valley. But the climate is less severe, for the trees shield the living community from the coldest winter winds and from the full effect of summer heat. While a shaded thermometer in an open field may range from 35 degrees below zero to 103 above, the average temperature in the woodlands is less extreme: seldom much below zero, or above 70 degrees on a summer day. Thoreau may have been consciously relying on this fact when he built his cabin in the woods, where he could reduce his own life to the greatest possible simplicity. Not only was fuel close at hand, but he benefited by the climatic insulation the forest everywhere provides.

The shores of Walden and the undisturbed parts of the Oyster River valley are naturally wooded because they receive a generous amount of moisture from the clouds in all seasons. If this precipitation came uniformly on the drainage basin of our river, it would average three and a third inches every month. Usually it varies from this average only about half an inch each way, with the heaviest rains in April and September, the dryest weather in May and November. Or so the weather records over the last sixty years indicate.

The forest conserves this moisture and keeps its own humidity high. Life, in consequence, is spread through more tiers among the trees than anywhere else around. From deep in the soil, into which the giants extend their

88

heavy roots to save themselves from toppling in a windstorm, to the highest branch displaying foliage to the sun, each kind of woodland animal has some favorite level. Some, such as the squirrels, climb skilfully and commute vertically by day. Their travels are familiar. Others, even less fitted than ourselves for scrambling up and down, run on the ground. Deer and fox, hare and skunk, are horizontal commuters. They keep open countless paths in the boundary undergrowth between the meadow and the forest.

Through the larger trails we can shoulder our way and stand below the interlaced branches, realizing that here the tall woody plants have won in their perennial contest with wind and fire, grass and browsing animals. For a century or more their victory has been complete, permitting once slender trunks to expand into great pillars holding up the forest canopy. Ordinary winds can ruffle only the topmost foliage. Ordinary fires char just the rough outermost layer of bark. In the filtered sunlight on the ground, grass cannot grow.

Few plants on the forest floor attract the hare and deer. Neither of these animals could subsist long on fronds of ferns, scaly stalks of club moss, shrubby lichens, tough bracket fungi, or the soft mosses that upholster each big rock and fallen tree. Neither animal can digest the cellulose and lignin of the wood itself. Even the resilient carpet of glossy wintergreen and red-dotted partridgeberry is not for them. The spectacular spring flowers—hepaticas, anemones, wild lilies of the valley, and moccasin orchids—offer no reliable nourishment. Instead, what the forest offers the deer and the hare (and the fox that follows in their tracks) is chiefly a hiding place. It is a sort of spacious outdoor cave, one within a reasonable distance of their feeding grounds

89

The spring wildflowers of the valley's woodlands have many names and are common over a wide geographic range. Some people call them wood anemone, mayflower, nimbleweed, wild cucumber, or just "wood flower."

along the woodland border or in the meadow under the stars. Each night they venture forth, each dawn they return to places of concealment. They may even lose a pursuer in the deadly game of hide-and-seek among the trees.

To be able to find nourishment as well as shelter among the regular products of the trees is the mark of the true denizen of the forest. The choice is limited largely to leaves and woody parts, living or dead, and only animals with special adaptations can eat these materials. Nevertheless, a remarkable assortment of creatures have such adaptations. New green leaves in the topmost tier are fare for caterpillars, the larvae of moths we may never see. The redstart and the black-burnian and other warblers that prefer to hunt high above the ground eat the caterpillars—thereby dining

90

Trailing arbutus is more than just another "mayflower." Its fragrant pinkish bells appear early on a woody vine as much as fifteen feet long; it is commonest in the sandy evergreen woodlands of New England.

on leaves at second hand. Halfway down the tree, nuthatches pry into crevices of rough bark for other kinds of insects as food for themselves and their nestlings. Among the litter of dead leaves and branches on the soil, ovenbirds and various thrushes hop in search of still other insects, as well as snails and worms. In the litter itself, myriad animals of small size (as well as bacteria and fungi) feed on the fallen debris and speed the processes of decay. And as much as ten feet underground, immature cicadas suck the juices from tree roots. So long as the forest lasts, all of these amenities can be counted on every year: new leaves, new bark around new wood, new dead leaves and branches on their way to becoming soil, and new roots spreading from every live tree.

The forest fungi

Of all the life in the woodlands, only the trees and other green plants, the insects and the birds attract the

91

casual eye. Most of the abundant agents of decay are too small and inconspicuous. Yet some of them do draw attention as soon as they begin producing spores to be carried by the wind. After a good rain at any time from spring until fall, the forest floor erupts with short-lived mushrooms of many kinds. Each fungal parasol thrusts aside the layers of leaf mold, and admits air into the soil. Then it spreads its cap, perhaps seven inches across and six inches above the ground.

The forms of these mushrooms seem endless. Their colors range from deep red to bright yellow and smoky gray. Some of the most beautiful are also the most dangerous. The dusky white *amanita* known as the

From the woodland floor, deadly amanita *mushrooms rise. Their orange tops are flecked with ivory-colored scales.*

"destroying angel," which rises from a conspicuous cup, is our most poisonous fungus. The fly amanita is even more attractive, with its yellow or deep orange top flecked with angular white patches. For most animals it too is deadly, although red squirrels, chipmunks, and many fungus-eating insects eat it with impunity.

Among the fungi of the woodlands, the bizarre is actually a commonplace, leading to all manner of picturesque names. Firm dark growths pointing upward from well-rotted logs are "dead man's fingers." Soft, sticky folds of yellow material on the same logs are "witches' butter." Ivory-colored shelves with thin white gills below, spreading from the side of a dead tree, are "oyster mushrooms." On the soil or on the wet, crumbling remains of rotted logs are "coral fungi"—branching growths in pink or orange, red or yellow. Even a single fallen twig may bear several thin-walled miniature cups that are brilliant scarlet within and flesh-colored outside; these are the "scarlet cups"—spectacular enough to be worth taking home as decorations, if only they did not quickly shrivel and blacken as their spores are discharged. Most of these and still smaller fungi are able to digest the lignins of wood—substances that are resistant even to bacterial decay.

Among woodland fungi the "sponge mushrooms" or morels, which rise as much as six inches above the forest floor, excel all others in food value. Unfortunately, they are never common, and are less substantial than they look. At the center of each morel is a large cavity; its outer surface is raised deceptively in tawny intersecting ridges.

Among fungi the longest-lived are those that grow on dead and living trees, particularly on the hardwoods.

93

These are the bracket fungi, which extend outward from the tree trunk and add to their rims and lower surfaces every year a new zone from which spores are shed. Thin leathery brackets crowded together in serried ranks are distinctly marked with eccentric bands in greenish gray, which show how many years the shelf has been expanding. Thick woody brackets live even longer. A few in our valley are as much as two feet across and four or five inches thick. The doomed trees on which they began their life took many years to die. This gave them a head start, for it is a rare hardwood log that takes twenty years to decay after death. Yet some of the brown-topped bracket fungi reach an age of twenty-five years, as can be proved by counting the new decks of spore-producing tissue added each summer.

Not all of the fungi in the woodlands assist in the process of decay. Some go into partnership with minute green algae and form lichens. They encrust the bare rocks and the bark of living trees. Others grow upon stumps and soil. A few have earned common names known to people who enjoy the miniatures among plants. "Indian matches" or "British soldiers" are little green-gray lichens whose erect branches end in bright red knobs. "Pyxie cups" lack the red color, and resemble diminutive ice-cream cones no more than an inch high. Often the two are mixed together around the drying rim of a rotting stump, as though someone had set out an elfin garden in the forest. Discovering them is one of the rewards of focusing on the unpretentious denizens of a plant community where man himself is dwarfed by trees.

Birds among the shadows

The fallen logs and branches, the rising new growth of mushrooms and trees, all furnish a wealth of hiding places for forest birds and for the small animals they eat. Most of the birds are well adapted to escape notice even when in plain sight, by having feathers colored in shades that match the woodland browns or distract the eye from seeing enough of the body outline at once to recognize its owner. But birds that move about on the forest floor or that utter distinctive calls attract attention to themselves. They add an element of mystery to the world of the trees, and lure any naturalist to match up an actual bird with the sounds he hears.

Each rustling between the fern clumps tells of some creature among the leaves. But scratching sounds alone tell no one which bird it is—if, indeed, it is a bird at all. If the noise-maker is approached with care, we may discover a towhee, or one of the thrushes, or perhaps a fox sparrow on migration through the valley. Each of these forest birds is an expert acrobat, able to leap upward and kick the loose leaves with both feet at once, then snatch any snail or insect that is exposed.

Early in the morning or toward sunset, any of these scratchers except the fox sparrow is likely to identify itself by a clear song. The oversized sparrow, which is streaked in cinnamon-brown, saves its bell-like melodies for its nesting grounds in northern Canada and Alaska. The others produce delightful harmonies and intriguing call notes that are as distinctive as the color patterns of the birds themselves.

Almost anyone can imitate the towhee well enough to get the bird to answer and approach. But it would take quite a whistler to mimic successfully the complex songs of the thrushes. Now that scientists have recorded and analyzed thrush calls, we have even better reason to respect these vocalists. They sing true to musical scales, and can produce as many as four different tones at once.

95

Often the sparrow hawk perches at the edge of the woodland between forays over the meadow. It dines on grasshoppers and other large insects more often than on meadow mice, and on mice more often than on sparrows.

The wood thrush is a master of unhurried silver phrasings, grouping them in seemingly endless combinations, with a voice so full and clear that no note goes unheard. By comparison, the hermit thrush is a shy performer, who sings the same piquant melody in one key after another. We find ourselves holding our breath the better to follow its cadenzas and arpeggios. Remarkably, the hermit closely resembles, both in the form of its body and in its inconspicuous brown plumage, the other chief contenders for the honor of being the world's most accomplished feathered vocalist: the nightingale of Europe, and the shama thrush of India.

The sounds, the shadows, the animals and plants in our valley's woodlands correspond closely to those in other similar parts of northeastern America. The wood pewee, who calls from a high bare branch between swoops after insects between the trees, recalls forests of oak and pine north of Lake Ontario. A lilt in the voice of a thrush sometimes takes us back to a parklike beech wood we loved in Pennsylvania. The churring note of a red squirrel can be heard in woodlands from coast to coast, almost anywhere in the northern half of the continent. Once the little squirrel with the white eye rings and flirty tail has been accepted as an interesting neighbor, it seems to be just an excitable friend wherever it is met. Probably it has longer established rights in our woodland than most other mammals, for its ancestors helped in planting the acorns and nuts from which the oaks and hickories grew.

A family of screech owls watches from a tree branch. The young emerge after dusk to wait on a branch until their parents return with a mouse or a katydid or a big earthworm. Screech owls rely on their big eyes and keen ears to guide them to living food.

One of the most retiring among the loud-voiced callers in the woodlands of our valley—the whippoorwill— seems equally at home among the trees of New England or Florida or New Mexico or Costa Rica. Wherever we hear its insistent note, we quickly feel at home. But by day anywhere, the bird crouches lengthwise on a horizontal limb, where it passes for a lumpy bit of bark. In darkness it often perches crosswise, and there produces cries so loud that no other noise of the forest can be heard above them. At close range the sound is preceded by a little catching note, as though the bird were sucking in a last gasp of air before releasing the penetrating *WHIPpoorWILL!* And all the time the whippoorwill is listening for distant birds of its own kind, for any snap of twig or crunch of leaf that might reveal the nearness of some predator in darkness. While calling, the whippoorwill never isolates itself from audible messages.

Eventually the insistent *WHIP*ping ceases, and the bird flies off. It is a vertical commuter, rising into the night sky to wing along with its big bewhiskered mouth open, trawling the air above the forest for moths and other flying insects. No May beetle is too big. Even the largest moths fall prey, their scaly wings fluttering back to earth while their bodies join the mosquitoes and gnats that are gathered in during each collecting trip.

At nesting time, the whippoorwills descend to ground level and lay their two eggs on the bare earth or atop a few leaves in a shallow depression of the soil. How the parents manage to find their young in the darkness remains a mystery. That they somehow do so is shown by the speed with which whippoorwill chicks grow fat on the rich protein food brought back and regurgitated by the parents.

By day a nesting whippoorwill is in danger of being stepped on. We remember one clutch of eggs that escaped this calamity as we walked along a woodland trail only because the parent almost struck our faces with her wings as she leaped into the air at the last possible moment. Each egg bore an irregular scrawl of dark markings, and blended perfectly with the surrounding forest litter even while resting on a couple of saucering oak leaves. Later, while we watched from our own crude concealment behind some shrubbery, the whippoorwill returned and settled a few inches from her eggs. Laboriously, as though each step would be her last, she worked her shortlegged way to the clutch and got her breast feathers over her charges. Her own markings destroyed the outline of her body, making her all but invisible again.

Possibly a whippoorwill finds an opportunity to pick up insects that are walking past even while it is incubating eggs or brooding its young. Sometimes the crops of these birds contain caterpillars and the cocoons of ants, which the adult ants carry about. Neither could be taken in flight. To this extent, a whippoorwill might lay claims to being a true denizen of the woodlands—eating as well as sleeping, singing, and nesting there.

We worry about nesting whippoorwills whenever the rustling noises we trace on the forest floor prove to come from dry leaves pushed abruptly aside by a foraging shrew, the smallest of warm-blooded mammals. A shrew that weighs barely half an ounce, measures three inches from the tip of its short tail to the end of its pointed nose, will tackle an animal weighing three times as much. It can kill a snake two feet long. We wonder what happens when a shrew comes close to a whippoorwill.

99

It is possible that the bird has no odor to alert the shrew. Some scientists believe that the whippoorwill quickly gathers her eggs or newly hatched young into her capacious mouth, and flies off with them to some safer part of the forest. Perhaps the bird we disturbed had no time to perform this trick, and really did not notice us when she returned to her eggs. The next day we visited the nest site but found it empty—with no trace of shell anywhere around.

In the swampy forest

In wetter parts of the woodland, where dense alders grow from the black muck, we look for woodcocks nesting on the ground. For about three weeks each spring, these birds take their chances with the voracious shrews while incubating three or four buffy eggs. Their downy young too would be tasty morsels for any predator. The chicks, however, are experts at immobility. They freeze in whatever position they happen to be when the hen bird whirrs vertically upward from the forest floor, distracting an intruder and temporarily deserting her brood. Once, when a mother woodcock rose before us in this way, we hunted until we found her tan-and-brown youngsters. Two of them stood statuesquely on their short legs with long beaks straight ahead. Two more lay on their backs with feet and bills pointing stiffly at us, just where they had tumbled when their parent left. Only their bright eyes, set high in the top of the head, followed our movements as though to measure how well their ruse was succeeding. If we had concealed ourselves behind a big stump and watched until the mother bird returned, we might have seen her carry off her babies one at a time, clutched between her thighs. She attends to these rescue

100

missions without any help from her mate, for he deserts her as soon as the eggs hatch.

In the wet soil among the alders, the woodcocks drill circular holes with their extraordinary beaks. For as much as three inches downward they probe the muck for earthworms and grubs, opening the flexible tips of the beak enough to seize these favorite foods. While engrossed in this task, their eyes still give them almost panoramic vision. At the slightest disturbance, a woodcock flies straight up to treetop height and there pauses ever so briefly. Almost like a hummingbird it hovers momentarily before darting off in a straight line to some other bit of alder swamp.

To propel its plump body, a woodcock beats its short wings furiously. Despite its short tail, it is well adapted to dodging branches, even while traveling through our woodland at better than twelve miles an hour. To have one come directly at you, perhaps five feet above the path, is almost as unnerving as to be in the way of a small airplane. We cannot resist dodging, although from experience we know that the bird will whiz past us.

In spring, the male woodcock waits to court his mate until the twilight hours after sunset or before dawn, or under the glow of a full moon. Only then does this shy bird put on his sky dance and produce his strange music. Time after time he repeats his exhibition, spiraling upward from her side, circling at a height of about two hundred feet, then zigzagging downward again in a dizzy plunging flight to alight and strut before her on the ground.

A low meadow in our valley, between two swampy bits of woodland, is a favorite courting ground. But if we are to approach without interrupting his display, it

101

is essential to wait until the male bird whirrs upward at a sharp angle from the clearing. As soon as he begins circling in the luminous sky above the forest, we walk quickly into the field, the better to see and hear. While he circles the trees, he sends back an eerie sound to his mate on the ground. It combines a high-pitched twittering with an intermittent buzzing, produced by three special feathers on each wing. Without warning the display changes, and the bird plummets toward the earth. Leveling off directly above his mate, he circles the meadow to alight beside her. Among the shrubs he is quickly lost to view. But we hear his nasal *peent* call time after time as he struts before her, seeking her approval. Then up he goes again, continuing his courtship until darkness (or daylight), or some disturbance on the ground, puts an end to the twilight peace he requires for his dance.

By day, when our eyes are more useful in looking toward the ground, we return to the woodcock's courting area. Shrews forage there for the same kinds of worms and soil insects as the birds take. The shrews, however, seem more versatile than the woodcocks, for they devour also snails, woodlice, spiders, and some vegetable material. Only a few animals of a size a shrew could manage escape attack, apparently because they are poisonous or evil-tasting: the armored millipedes, which feed directly on decaying foliage, and the harvestmen ("daddy longlegs"), which hold their compact bodies cantilevered on eight thread-slender legs.

Shrews consume daily more than three times their own weight, chiefly in meaty prey found on the soil or just beneath its surface. This great variety is in foods that can be digested quickly. Yet most of the energy obtained is soon lost, either in the vigorous exercise of hunting for more, or as heat radiated from the warm little body

102

despite its soft coat of dense short fur. Just to stay alive, a shrew that scarcely balances a fifty-cent coin in weight must find and engulf every day summer and winter, food equivalent to a hundred and ten honeybees. No other animal of our woodlands needs food so desperately.

So intent are shrews in seizing every bit of meat in reach that they often ignore commotions that could give them warning. Probably a shrew's vision is too poor for the animal to see as much detail at a distance of two feet as we notice at twenty. Certainly these little mammals seem unaware of us in the Oyster River valley until we are within a yard or so. Perhaps this preoccupation with hunting accounts for the occasional shrews that venture beyond the woodlands into open country, where they become easy prey for owls and hawks, foxes and house cats, which watch and listen intently there.

As though in compensation, shrews pair off two or three times a summer. They build little mounds of fallen leaves as nurseries in the forest, and in each raise a family of eight or nine youngsters. The newborn shrews are hairless and no bigger than honeybees. But so rich is the mother's milk that the babies double their weight every few days. Soon they share the insects and grubs brought to the nursery by the attentive male. Before long they show their independence by going off alone, ready to attack any armored beetles bigger than they are, or even to fight to the death with others of their own kind.

Workers in the soil

Most of the living things in the forest live within reach of the shrew, but it can use as food only those of the right size—neither too big nor too small. The majority of animals in the soil are minute. Most of them engulf bacteria, fungi, and algal cells in the water-filled spaces between the mineral particles, or inside organic structures such as leaves. Unicells are especially abundant. With them are hordes of wheel animalcules, roundworms, and flatworms; many of these occur the world over in this limited habitat. They are the essential food for predatory spider mites and springtail insects which, although barely big enough to see, may number as many as forty-five hundred to the square foot. Tiny pseudoscorpions capture the springtails and the mites, seizing them in outstretched pincers and holding them firmly while draining their juices. Small ants capture the mites and minute insects, carrying them back as trophies to the nest.

This multitude depends for life upon food that drops to earth like an intermittent rain, totaling about half a pound per square foot each year. It consists of plant debris and of animal wastes and remains. By successive stages of decomposition, the material passes through the bodies of the various soil organisms in sequence. It provides each with nourishment, and at the same time becomes progressively simpler chemically until it is reduced to molecules that can be absorbed by the roots of trees. Without the soil's living things, this sequence would break down and the forest be choked with its own wastes.

So many animals scurry about in the upper soil that it retains its open texture and serves as a way station between the aerial and the subterranean strata of the woodland. It is a special habitat, one that—like the forest as a whole—stays cooler than the air above in summer, and warmer by many degrees in winter. Usually it is doubly insulated. Dead leaves form one layer. Snow in winter or the large plants and trees above in summer provide a second layer. Consequently it is a place of almost continuous activity, albeit on a miniature scale, throughout the year.

The whole pattern of life in the forest floor reflects a discipline of permanence in the trees above. Earthworms, which drag down and devour the rotting foliage or engulf the loose soil itself (including its mineral particles), may reach an age of ten years if they are lucky enough never to venture to the surface where a shrew is hunting. On the deep roots of the living trees, cicada nymphs explore for thin places in the bark. Through these they slide their stylet mouthparts and suck the tree juices. Some of these cicadas become the oldest insects in the world, yet only in their last few weeks of life do they emerge into the sunshine among the treetops. Some of the trees they rest on may have been mere seedlings when these same individual cicadas hatched from the egg.

Each cicada nymph keeps its own internal record of the years spent feeding underground. Only one brood matures to shrill siren calls each summer in the Oyster River valley. During some years, more cicadas mature than in others. Brood X, which will reappear again in 1987, is the largest. When last this brood emerged from the ground, as many as eighty-four holes were opened to the square foot over a twenty-foot circle under a fair-sized tree, each hole made by a separate individual. This one tree had nourished more than thirty-three thousand cicadas of just one brood without apparent harm. Sixteen other broods to come were still feeding in the ground.

Life in the treetops

Except when a windstorm knocks a few hundred slow-moving insects to the ground, we tend to forget what spectacular numbers of them are feeding on the foliage out of sight in the crowns of the forest trees. This top tier of our woodlands is home to some of the most re-markable caterpillars—creatures reaching a length of four or five inches. Several kinds show special versatility in accepting the resinous needles of coniferous trees as readily as the softer foliage of the broad-leafed types. As moths, however, they show no real interest in any food, although from time to time they uncoil their watch-spring tongues and take a sip of dew.

No less than five of the giant moths that have been famous ever since Gene Stratton Porter wrote her stories of the *Limberlost* are creatures of the treetops in our valley. Two of them, the elegant cecropia and the fawn-colored polyphemus, rarely come down from their lofty feeding sites to spin a cocoon preparatory to the trans-formation into a broad-winged moth. Rather, they tie their distinctive cocoons firmly to the high branches; their caterpillars are seldom seen on the ground. The larva of the pastel green luna moth, on the other hand, generally descends and spins its cocoon among fallen leaves that will be covered by winter's snow. The cater-pillars of the handsome imperial moth and of the royal walnut moth come down too, each of them to spend a few weeks as a naked pupa in the loose soil before emerging to winged adulthood. We often carry home full-grown caterpillars and luna-moth cocoons to watch.

By experience we have learned never to count our moths before they spread their wings. More than half of the cocoons and of the plump caterpillars conceal internal parasites—the young of particular species of wasps which devour the moth larvae or pupae. The way of life of these denizens of our woodland differs in no important detail from those the patient Fabre watched in his cabbage caterpillars. Each parasite is a little white grub, "neatly segmented. . . . It does not chew, it sucks, it takes dis-creet sips at the moisture all around it. . . . Nor does aught to the outside betray any havoc within." The hosts

106

"expire, quite softly, not of any wounds, but of anemia, even as a lamp goes out when the oil comes to an end." It is wasps that emerge after the host has been killed.

Other denizens of the treetops are often larger, but seldom disclose their presence. If a pair of crows builds a nest high in the forest, the birds keep silent. When the crows desert their nest and one of the great owls remodels it as a platform for round white eggs that will hatch fuzzy youngsters, enormous of eye and appetite, only the slightest sounds penetrate the woodlands to alert us on the ground. Even the cries of the young birds, as they beg excitedly for food brought back by the parents, tend to be high-pitched hisses we do not recognize as having an animal origin. More often than not these sounds are absorbed by the layers of leaves before reaching the low levels in the forest. In consequence, our New England woodlands are impressively peaceful, particularly after the nesting birds settle down to raising families.

Nature's lumbermen

At every level, the forest gives an impression of immense stability. This year's shade resembles that of last year and of the year before. For decades, perhaps centuries, each tree trunk has been situated exactly where it stands today. Yet trees are mortal, and only their branch tips are young. Cuttings from new branches can be induced to take root, reproducing the original tree in specific detail with full fidelity. But all of the older parts, however inconspicuously, show signs of age. In one great limb after another, each tree eventually loses out. It no longer can drown insect invaders in a vigorous rush of sap, or repel the insidious threads of fungi entering through cracks in its trunks and branches.

Certain kinds of animals excel in detecting signs of senility in a tree. But it is hard to be sure which comes first: the insects or the fungi. Both rank as nature's lumbermen, but generally neither is visible from the outside until the tree is richly populated beneath the loosening bark. By the time a big woodpecker noisily hammers a hole through to the insects it can hear working in the wood, the damage is done. The tree may be ready to collapse, and to contribute its remains to the small agents of decay in the forest soil.

In the woodlands of our valley we sometimes occupy a grandstand seat at the wrecking of a long-dead giant, when the biggest of our woodpeckers—the crow-sized pileated—sets to work. But this is the end of the show, the grand finale. Only by piecing together a string of less spectacular observations can we see how the stage is set for the natural removal of an old tree, making a place for a young one.

The steps toward a big tree's downfall follow a definite pattern. At an ever brisker pace the nourishing substances stored within the tree are converted into pale, thread-thin strands of fungi and into insects of myriad kinds. Small insects come first, then larger ones, and finally the carpenter ants—our largest ants—which, soon after they colonize the tree, attract the pileated woodpecker.

Evidence of the first steps is visible where the bark begins separating from the wood. Here the tree is already dead. Otherwise the space between the bark and the wood is occupied by a thin sheath of growing cells. They add to the tree's girth the new conducting tubes of sapwood, which carry water to the leaves, and also the new tubes in the inner bark, which transport food toward the roots. This delicate sheath is a prime target for any insect

108

or fungus, since its cell walls are thin and soft, its cell contents rich in nutrients.

Where the bark tears easily from over a tree's woody heart, the surface of the wood is often channeled shallowly—engraved in an intricate branching design. Opposite the place where all of the channels in a group come together, the matching piece of bark is almost sure to be perforated by a small circular hole. This is the work of a male engraver beetle, an insect perhaps less than an eighth of an inch in length. With his jaws the beetle bores inward to the soft nutritious cells, and there excavates a group of short radiating tunnels in which to install a harem of mates. Each female lays a few eggs, from which small grubs hatch out. Every grub begins chewing away, and filling the passageway behind it with a frass of undigested wood. Somehow the beetle grubs manage to tunnel on roughly parallel courses, destroying more and more of the soft tissue of the tree, and producing the pattern from which the beetles get their name.

When many engraver beetles manage to invade the same tree, the multiple channels cut by their young are almost sure to kill it by girdling. Sometimes the exit holes made by hundreds of engraver beetles are visible, giving the bark the appearance of having received a shotgun blast of fine lead pellets at close range. Often the emerging beetles carry with them live spores of fungi, which germinate within the next old tree to be attacked and eventually destroy it—even if the beetles fail to do so. The famous "Dutch" disease of the American elm is carried in this way. Already it has killed a great many of the tall elms whose graceful branches spread over the wetter and more open parts of the woodlands in our valley.

In some ways it seems incongruous that such small beetles should be able to kill a big tree. Engraver beetles are of a size that appeals to a chickadee or a warbler, or to a six-inch downy woodpecker, but not to larger birds. Bigger woodpeckers feed on bigger insects. But once a tree is killed, the bigger beetles come. They transform the dead wood into more beetles, and more food for woodpeckers.

Only certain beetles possess the adaptations required for feeding within a tree. That so many different kinds participate in the march of new attackers is mainly an indication of the enormous variety among beetles. These hard-bodied creatures are the most successful of all insects; they account for nearly half of the kinds of insects on earth, while insects as a whole make up about three-fourths of all the kinds of animal life. America north of the Rio Grande, has three times as many kinds of beetles as there are kinds of birds in the whole world. No wonder the bark of a dead tree in our valley often conceals members of better than a dozen beetle families!

With so many kinds of beetles, it is not surprising that most of them are specialists. Actually, some of the beetles found under bark in winter do no damage to the tree. This protected site is a favorite place for the familiar ladybird beetles to hibernate in. Dozens of them may cling side by side, often in company with large darkling beetles or with some of the many kinds that feed on the fungi attacking the wood. But in summer, the engraver beetles, metallic woodborers, and longicorns are frequently active on the outside of the bark. They and their larvae cut into the wood itself, making tunnels as much as three-eighths of an inch in diameter, through the hardest wood. Only those with strong jaws can bore so powerfully. Powderpost beetles nibble daintily, and

110

specialize on very dry wood. Stag beetles and various of the big scarabs choose only wet and crumbly parts of the tree, where fungi have softened the structure of the wood. Still other beetles are there to feed on beetles. The smaller of our two species of gray-bodied click beetles—the one with handsome eyespots on its back—is like its active young in entering the tunnels cut by other insects in a tree, and in dining on whichever wood-eater chances to be there.

Of all the insects in an old tree, the beetles are the most varied and numerous. They riddle the wood with their tunnels. But only an occasional beetle larva is so near the outside of a tree that a woodpecker can open a small hole through the bark and spear the individual insect on its barbed tongue. The other beetles are too far into the solid trunk, and too scattered to be available to birds.

At this stage in the deterioration of a dead tree, we can glimpse further ways in which the birds of the forest too are specialists. All of the woodpeckers that drill for insects through the bark have spongy tissue between the strong beak and the heavy skull, as a barrier against vibrations. With stiff tail feathers that serve as a prop for the body, each bird grasps the bark with its specially adapted feet—two toes up and two down. But the downy opens only a small circular hole—a conical cavity to the insect it seeks; observant Virginia Eifert likens the sound it makes to the tapping of a typewriter. The hairy woodpecker, which is more than half again as large as the downy, chips out a square opening and takes larger insects. The noise it makes is more like a riveting machine. There is little competition between the two woodpeckers, and neither of them has the physical ability to accomplish what the big pileated can do.

The work of the pileated, which is the most spectacular display in our woodlands, must wait until the carpenter ants arrive and ready the tree for the banquet. These energetic black ants hunt for beetles and beetle larva, following them into their winding tunnels and devouring them, or bringing them back in pieces to feed young ants. Even in raising their brood the hunting ants show great efficiency. They excavate huge galleries under the bark on the sunny side of the tree, where their incubators are warmed each day and the young ants speedily develop.

Any big dead tree is likely to have a separate colony of carpenter ants. It begins with a mated pair at the end of their nuptial flight, when they discover a tree well supplied with beetles. At some opening in the bark the two ants snap off their wings and enter. Between meals the female starts a family and tends the first brood herself. Before long, several dozen worker ants have matured and taken over the duties of nursemaids. Some of the young workers explore the tree systematically for more living food. Others excavate galleries for another brood, dumping crumbs of wood, one at a time, from some opening through the bark, until only a skeleton of woody struts remains.

Now the stage is set, and our pileated woodpecker makes the most of it. Through the Oyster River valley this primeval bird flashes in broad swooping flight, every white marking aglisten, to alight on the old tree. With brilliant red crest bobbing and powerful beak hammering away, the bird tosses out fragments of bark and great showers of light-colored chips. Seemingly with a flair for showmanship, the big bird chisels out a rectangular hole directly into the ants' nest. Then, with the delicacy of a lady spearing olives at a cocktail party buffet, the pileated thrusts its sharp tongue into the

112

cavities and picks out the ants and their young, one at a time.

Some of the openings made by the giant woodpecker are veritable canyons in the tree, perhaps three feet long, and from six to eight inches in depth and breadth. The bird sometimes reaches its whole head and shoulders into the excavation. Yet the woodpecker never finds every ant in any tree. Many of the insects escape down their own corridors or into beetle holes, and regroup to make a fresh start with the colony. The old tree still harbors many beetles—more meals for ants—and more ants for woodpeckers. But gradually the wood is converted into insects and crumbs. A bear may finally demolish the tree, to reach the ants and beetles in its own heavy-pawed way. Bacteria and fungi in the soil complete the dissolution.

The pileated seems to typify the spirit of tree country more than any other bird of our woodlands. Its call, loud and commanding, fairly rings through the forest. Fortunately, the pileated has not yet gone the way of this country's only other large crested bird with a special taste for ants—the ivory-billed woodpecker of the South. But its numbers have been reduced in our valley and elsewhere in America, through man's habit of harvesting mature trees before they age and die, thus becoming suitable as feeding stations or nest sites. These changes affect the welfare of the forest too, for trees that fall and rot naturally make ideal nurseries for new tree seedlings. The seeds take root in the damp moss that grows on the fallen log, and the new roots gain mineral nutrients more reliably from the decaying trunk than from the upper layers of nearby soil.

The holes cut so expertly, with every corner squared, are another contribution by the pileated woodpecker to

113

other animals of the woodland. Small owls of the forest, such as the saw-whet and the boreal, are chronically in need of better housing. They take up residence in cavities hewed by the giant woodpecker. Raccoons, or a family of the weasel-like pine martens, can use a large hole as a den. A nest deserted by a pileated is a far drier haven than any tree hole where a big branch has given way and let rain soak into the dead wood, thus encouraging destructive fungus rots. The more available holes there are, in fact, the better the woodland can maintain variety in its animal life.

To meet some of the hole-dwellers in dead and dying trees, it is best to explore between the trees after dark. The most thoroughly nocturnal mammal in America is the flying squirrel, an inhabitant of tree holes, preferably those that are barely more than cup-sized. Through the day and twilight hours, these gentle squirrels hide away from the light so consistently that their presence in the forest is generally overlooked. But at night they peer from their places of concealment, take careful aim, and launch themselves on the furry gliding membranes that extend between the two legs on each side. Silently, a squirrel planes to the trunk of another tree, steering with its flattened tail. At the last moment it flicks the tail, to land safely head upward on the bark.

Sometimes we wonder whether we should not ask the owner of a woodland for permission to make more tree holes in it. Forest animals suffer from a real housing shortage. Today's glades are all too neat, too parklike. Even in a sanctuary area, the custodians are likely to remove any tree uprooted by a hurricane, or one that dies and might crush others in its fall. Gone are the hollow upright trees that used to house thousands of chimney swifts; these birds, however, proved adaptable enough to adopt the man-made cavities from which they get their name. Gone are the big hollow stubs in which a bear could take shelter from the winter storms. Gone too are the horizontal hollow logs on which a cock ruffed grouse can drum in mating time, standing stiffly erect and beating his wings against the loosening bark. Gone are the truly mature forests, where the decay of old trees is a normal part of life, and where animals find food, housing, and resonators close together.

These changes in the woodlands help make us safe from bears and other wild animals while wandering in darkness through our valley. No bear or cougar or timber wolf is likely to surprise us. Like the wild turkeys and the passenger pigeons, these mammals were eliminated long before many of the trees around us rose from the seed. Our greatest hazard now would be to stumble on a porcupine, or to collide head-on with a family of striped skunks. These animals too would avoid a close encounter if given half a chance.

Even the possibility of meeting a porcupine among the hemlocks in our valley has shrunk surprisingly in the last few years. Scarcely was the ink dry on newspaper discussions of how best to rid the orchards and forests of excess porcupines when the natural balance of nature began asserting itself. Some of the quill-bearers were eliminated by means of poisoned apples placed in their winter dens. A few were killed for a small bounty payment. But the principal change came through an increase in the number of fishers, mammals which are the arch-destroyers of porcupines. For a while the change was scarcely noticed, because the weasel-like fishers prowl chiefly at night when few men roam the woods. And few people sought fishers, for they had become so rare that by the 1940s, when the market for their soft pelts suddenly collapsed, they were listed along with cougars as probably extinct in our part of New England. Yet, as the abandoned orchards and pastures grew up into forest land and the slow-moving porcupines increased in numbers as the prickliest of nature's lumbermen, the rare fishers grew less rare.

Although a fisher can grow to the size of a small fox and often resembles one, it is a skilful climber. A fisher follows a porcupine into the treetops, and induces its victim to descend to the ground. There the predator pounces quickly and rolls the porcupine onto its back, to reach the unprotected underside. Fishers hunt also in darkness for sleeping squirrels, and vary their diet with raccoons, the tan-and-white deer mice, and other warm-blooded animals. Once again fishers are competing for tree-hole dens in which to raise their young. Already in many areas they seem to have the porcupines under control, and to be saving thousands of trees from premature destruction.

The bog forest

To commune today with the life of the really distant past, we venture to the bottom of Spruce Hole. There grow the small black spruces, and a whole bogful of peat moss which harks back many thousands of years to the time when New England was being recolonized by plant life after the great Ice Ages. To reach the place we push through a stand of second-growth pines—trees still too young to have dropped their needleless, brittle lower branches although years have passed since these branches withered in the dense shade of the live interlacing tops. We call them the "turnstile woods," and through them we press eagerly to the bottom of Spruce Hole.

If, as we step into the bog forest, the little black-masked warbler known as the northern yellowthroat is singing to his mate on her nest, he provides a connection with the geological present. But we have actually left the earth behind, without any rocket to boost us. Underfoot is the dark, icy, tea-colored water that would be a big pond if sedges and mosses had not roofed it over during the past thousand years. The roofing vegetation quakes and sinks wherever we stand. In some places, if an arm is thrust to the elbow between the clumps of soft *Sphagnum* moss, the fingers and hand encounter only water of unknown depth. Alice must have felt the same sense of unreality when she stepped through the Looking Glass.

No ordinary plant can make a living in this unique bit of the valley, for the cold meltwater that collects there each spring is promptly poisoned by the acid products of decaying moss. Moss grows on moss, thrusting the older parts into the water. But the limited decay provides no soil that might contribute nitrogen-containing nutrients. Oxygen is almost absent in the water. Plants thrive under these conditions only by being unplantlike—requiring from their roots no real anchorage, no nourishment, and almost no moisture.

The black spruces and low-growing shrubs manage by being miserly with water. Their roots radiate horizontally and mesh together among the moss for mutual support. As we move about, the whole mesh vibrates and the nearest trees tilt crazily, their tops lashing back and forth with each footstep. Dead spruce cones and needles of earlier years are still in place; only the tops are green, like miniature Christmas trees above our heads. But we wade knee-deep in wiry branches of bog laurel and Labrador tea—a rhododendron adapted to bog life. Both have waxed leathery leaves curled at the edges in a way that reduces water loss from the air-pores below.
117

By looking even more carefully among the peat moss, we recognize spidery stems with small evergreen leaves that appear almost overwhelmed by the *Sphagnum*. They are wild cranberries, whose nodding, bell-like pink flowers in late spring are seldom seen, but whose tart scarlet fruits can be harvested in late summer in almost any bog of the northern hemisphere.

Scattered between the trees and shrubs we still find a few open places where sedges and orchids live amid the lumpy rug of peat moss. They succeed by being opportunists: growing rapidly, flowering, and even fruiting before the summer air begins to compete for water. Then they dry to dormancy and wait until another spring, when the snow melts and furnishes more unpoisoned moisture among their leaf bases. The sedges raise narrow grasslike spears above the moss from their triangular horizontal stems. Coarsest of them is the "wool-bearer" (*Eriophorum*), whose flowers and fruits on tall stalks are candylike tufts of long white hair, inviting the common name of "cotton grass."

To see the bog orchids in flower we go before the end of spring. Then only do they produce their beautiful solitary blooms atop tall slender stalks, or their graceful spikes of tiny pink, purple, or green blossoms that resemble snakes' heads. Their perfume is the rarest in our valley. Some of it is almost intoxicatingly sweet when inhaled at the peak of the brief flowering season. After that, only the shriveling stalk remains above the few leaves with thick bases down among the moss.

Late spring is the time when the carnivorous pitcher plants send up, to a height of two feet, their even stranger flowers. Their five purplish petals flap like flags in any breeze, while the vaselike leaves of each rosette are in their prime. This bog denizen, our largest insect-

118

With roots holding in the peat moss, the pitcher plants produce rosettes of strange vase-like leaves each holding as much as a cupful of water. Insects that alight or creep over the flaring hood are guided into the water by downpointing bristles.

119

eating plant, is highly adapted to trapping its own nitrogen-containing nutrients. Each leaf forms a separate pitcher, partly supported and partly hidden by the moss. Its open end, from five to eight inches above the center of the rosette, bears a flaring hood that directs rain into the leaf. Through the dark aperture, water can usually be seen cupped inside.

Occasionally, an ant or a beetle creeps onto the hood close to the pitcher mouth, and investigates the inviting glands along the red markings that suggest the big blood vessels in a rabbit's ear. A fly may alight, perhaps attracted by the glistening surface of the leaf or the odor of decay emanating from the open throat. It finds itself standing on fine curved bristles that point into the slippery, hairless gape of the pitcher. The ant and the beetle are guided by the same bristles, always downward, inward, toward the water. The fly turns parallel with the stiff hairs, but gains no solid footing that would permit it to spread its wings and escape. It too flounders into the pitcher mouth, and buzzes helplessly as it skids into the liquid trap. By digesting the drowned insects, the plant gains nutrients it cannot obtain from the sodden bog.

By bending low and examining each pitcher carefully, we can usually locate a few that contain live spiders and insects whose adaptations permit them to outwit the carnivorous plant. Of these, the spiders weave a web like an acrobat's safety net across the throat of the pitcher, where it will catch flies and beetles as they skid toward almost certain doom. The spider that spins the web—and not the plant—then benefits from the strange leaf.

Where no web forms a grating in a pitcher's throat, some of the world's most extraordinary mosquitoes buzz in and out like helicopters. Pitcher-plant mosquitoes lay their eggs within the leaf. Somehow their wrigglers

120

The pale wax-like flowers of Indian pipe push upward through the leaf litter of the woodland. The plant lacks green coloring, and gets its food from decaying remains of woody plants through the aid of special fungus partners.

survive in the digestive fluid while capturing from it particles of food. Few other inhabitants of the bog forest have so limited a place in which to raise their young, for these mosquitoes (which bite no one) are found only in intimate association with pitcher plants.

Spruce Hole is the last outpost of pitcher plants and their mosquitoes in our valley. But decade by decade, the forest of pines and maples, beech and hemlock is crowding in to shade them out. Already the edges of the bog are filled with plant debris—with peat—in which a tree bigger than a black spruce can get a firm roothold. Soon the place where today we can step into another world will be just a depression in the woodland. Given enough time, the climax forest can conquer all.

121

The Rhythm of the Seasons

People who live in naturally wooded parts of the North Temperate Zone have the special good fortune to know four seasons, not just the Bible's two. Few other regions of the world show so regular a series of climatic changes through the year. Nor were spring and fall named until about the time of Shakespeare. New Englanders went a step farther, and vindicated Thoreau's view that "the intellect is a cleaver." They cleft the year once more and asserted the existence of five seasons. But no one was quite sure whether the extra one—Mud—came before or after spring.

That in 1250 A.D. spring was unrecognized explains why the words of the most ancient song written with musical notes ("Sumer is icumen in, Lhude sing cuccu!") seems today to be such a poor observation. When the cuckoo sings loudly, summer isn't coming in at all. It's spring. The distinction had not yet been made in John Heywood's day, as is shown in one of his oft-quoted *Proverbes*, first printed in 1546: "One swallow maketh not summer." Swallows arrive at their northern nesting sites as soon as winter's chill abates and insects become active. Not just one, but all of them reach their destinations long before what in any modern interpretation would be the summer season.

In the Oyster River valley we need no almanac to remind us of the timetable nature is following. Summer spreads genially, without regard for equinoxes or other special moments. It means the succession of strawberries for shortcake, blueberries for pies, blackberries for jelly, and eventually tomatoes—green ones for relishes, red for catsup and salads, and yellow for special occasions.

Summer is bobolinks caroling over the meadow, and kingbirds perched on the telephone lines, ready to chase an insect or a crow. It is one brood of little wrens launched the last week in June, and another by mid-August. It is hummingbirds by day and hawk moths by night visiting the flowers with deep corollas, and bumble-bees attending the middle-sized blossoms that are too deep for the tongues of lesser bees. It is a family of groundhogs romping at the burrow mouth, watched over carefully by their mother—and watched too by a crouching weasel that has ranged over a hundred acres of meadow land in the past twenty-four hours and caught only nine mice.

In summer, the woodlands in the valley offer natural air-conditioning when the hot sun is high. If we walk to the river at midday we take the shadiest path. On each side of our feet the multitude of soil dwellers are active around the clock, making full use of the warmth while hastening the decay of organic matter. Among them are strange waxy roots cooperating with fungus strands while getting nourishment from rotting wood. All summer they spread in the soil, sending up at intervals pinkish-white stems, each with a solitary ghostly flower—the Indian pipe. At first they nod stiffly. Then, as the seeds begin to swell, the stems straighten out to become vertical, each tipped with a slender vase-shaped capsule. By this stage we tend to overlook the Indian pipes because they have blackened and shriveled, no longer contrasting with the forest floor. They are just the dry remains of a flowering plant that never possessed a bit of green.

The silence of minute creatures in the humus on the forest floor is matched by a deceptive quiet extending far up among the branches of the tall trees. So peaceful is the woodland that its animals might be suspected of having gone away. But high above the ground among the foliage, thousands of caterpillars are munching leaves. Beetles are boring into wood. Birds are inconspicuously searching for insects with which to feed their nestlings.

Close to the river in the woodland, we wander under the youngest of the tall white pines, and appreciatively touch the soft needles on their low branches. If it is the last week in June, the gentle jostling starts a silent cascade of yellow dust—the ripe pollen grains, each with two balloonlike wings that catch the slightest breeze. While the pines are shedding this summer gold, the water in the ponds and bays of the river is gilded with pollen. Winds and currents push it into swirling streaks close to shore, like brush marks of a Paul Bunyan turned artist.

In the forest soil along the river the abundant moisture favors the growth of seedling trees. Their summer foliage serves as a curtain, concealing from one another the

124

animals of the woodland and those of the water world. If the green curtain is quietly approached and slowly parted, surprises on both sides can be expected. For a few moments, a great blue heron standing motionless at the edge of the water may remain unaware of any intrusion. A mother wood duck, followed by half a dozen ducklings, is likely to continue tipping head downward, feeding in the shallows on duckweed and various water plants. Her young chase mosquito wrigglers and other small insects. But when the heron squawks in alarm and takes to his broad wings, to flap ponderously upriver, the mother duck at top speed marshals her family out of sight.

An almost endless variety of wild animals tend their young throughout the summer. Some merely lead the way. Others prepare nurseries for their babies. A few go to great lengths to distract attention from their little families. Along the marsh margins and over the dry uplands, the sandpipers and killdeers make use of every trick their instincts provide. If we come close to where their chicks crouch motionless, the parent bird puts on a conspicuous display—pretending that one wing is broken. When we turn and face in the opposite direction but do not move away from the unseen brood, the mother bird generally circles into view and again invites attention by crying loudly. A fox, which might be fooled by this ruse into following the parent bird, is equally ready to lead a dog by many a devious route away from the den in which her own pups are hidden.

Lesser creatures in our valley have their own way of caring for their young. Some provide both shelter and food, yet never see their young. To gather building materials, mud-dauber wasps come repeatedly to puddles in the meadow after a summer rain. Often they disturb honeybees and sulfur butterflies drinking there. But each mud-dauber is intent on just one errand: to scoop up a mouthful of mud. To get it she stands on long slender legs marked in black and yellow, and holds her body high. Off with the mud she flies to a stone wall or other firm support, where she can fashion the material into a series of tubular chambers for her brood. Into each cavity (which may be an inch long and a quarter of an inch in diameter) she pushes half a dozen spiders, all of them paralyzed with poison from her sting. Quickly she adds one fertile egg among these provisions, and seals the chamber with additional mud in the form of a firm door. The yellow larva that hatches inside the chamber must feed itself, grow, pupate, transform into an adult wasp, and then break out of the adobe prison which its mother has made. If it is a female, it emerges completely equipped with the instinctive ability to make an identical set of chambers for another brood of young—young it will never see.

Wherever there is a field of summer flowers, butterflies twinkle gaily among the wasps and bees, alighting, sipping, flitting everywhere. Atop a purple head of Joe Pye weed, several may rest at once. Each uncoils and recoils its long black tongue to probe after nectar into the depths of one floret after another. Butterflies with imaginative names, such as painted ladies, red admirals, anglewings, hairstreaks, and skippers, display their wings in the sun on leaves in plain view. Or they deposit a few eggs on the particular plants that serve as food for their caterpillars, then return to the flowers for more sugar water. A few, such as the delicate azure butterflies, go chiefly to specific flowers, where they lay their eggs and where later their caterpillars will eat the fruits. Most others sip at random, and give no clues to which plants

126

their caterpillars feed upon. Black swallowtails, which develop from caterpillars that feed on wild carrot, drink side by side with tawny fritillaries developed from larvae that feed on violet leaves.

In early summer at our latitude the butterfly's day is long, but the moths and the night birds have little darkness in which to be active. The sun sets in the northwest just before eight o'clock, and finally recedes far enough below the horizon for twilight to end officially at about twenty after ten. Three and a half hours later the sun begins once more to brighten the sky. It rises soon after four fifteen. No wonder the night herons are compelled to stalk for fish along the river bank in broad daylight, and underwing moths to flit like butterflies between the trunks of forest trees.

So much is going on at every hour all summer in our valley that the most complete almanac could not record the full details. Yet the wild things do meet their appointments with reasonable regularity. The late Aldo Leopold relied on his personal chronicle to report that each week from April until September, an average of ten different wild plants came into bloom. No one, he claimed, could keep watch on so many, or ignore them all either.

The events and the creatures of the meadows and woodlands show all degrees of provincialism. Some identify the countryside as definitely North American. Others are as characteristically New England. But the living things of the Oyster River, whether they be its duckweeds or water striders or caddis worms, resemble those to be found on ponds and slow streams all the way from the arctic tundra to the tropical rain forests. The English naturalist Thomas Belt first noticed this in the wilds of Nicaragua. He remarked that whenever his life in the remote parts of Central America made him lonesome, he had only to borrow a canoe and to paddle out on a broad river or a lake in order to feel at home again. The water lilies and dragonflies around him resembled so closely those he had known elsewhere as a boy that he could temporarily forget the tapirs and monkeys, the strange snakes and jungle vegetation along the shores.

This universality in the fresh waters of the world remains even toward the end of summer, when no water is running over the dam on the Oyster River. As in many another valley, the mat of duckweed completely bridges the bays and ponds, shutting out light and air. So tightly are the individual plants wedged together that a breeze capable of riffling open water into a sparkling semblance of life merely rocks the duckweed flakes a little, making them reflect a golden glitter over the dying vegetation below. The stalks of the pickerelweed are brown and broken, exposed by the low water with hanks of dead algae hanging forlornly from the stems that so proudly supported flowers.

Fall

Throughout the water world of the valley, no more swallows chitter in aerial acrobatics over the river and the millpond. Now that so few aquatic insects are emerging to become the food of swallows, the birds have left. The dabbling ducks, which tipped up to reach plants and small animals on the bottom all summer, can no longer find enough to eat. They and their maturing youngsters are winging southward. In the same direction, geese pass both day and night, honking high above the valley. Most of the migratory birds are in warmer regions before the autumn storms bring our river back to size, restoring the voice of the dam and the chatter of the riffles.

Long before the hard frosts come, repeated rains fill the ponds and wells, and put needed water into the soil. Then the chill winds abate. The sun brings back Indian summer, and the whirligigs join the striders in venturing out onto the surface film. Each night they prepare anew for cold weather, by creeping ashore into hiding places below fallen leaves. There the snow will come and insulate them from the winter.

At first, only a few scattered leaves on woodland trees show color. On the forest floor the green of ferns is transmuted to gold. Clusters of red fruit on bunchberry, and knobby red masses on the stalks of jack-in-the-pulpit, shine like lacquer. Where the paired flowers of partridgeberry opened there are now double scarlet fruits, joined more closely than Siamese twins. Solitary fruits of the same bright color hang below the wax-glossed leaves of wintergreen. Wild rose is a tangle of tiny red hips, like shoe buttons on short stems. And where bittersweet clambers over low-growing trees, the tan covers are ready to split from its fruits, revealing the brilliant orange-red within.

Even before the real autumn colors come, we recognize in winter buds that the hardwoods are prepared for cold and snow. Mushrooms and shelf fungi send out their last spores for the year. Most of the insects hide away in cocoons or survive as eggs, as able as the trees to stand the winter. On unseasonably warm days, only the mourning cloak butterfly and a few of the anglewings still flit about aimlessly. They brighten the woodlands, but are ready to creep back into crevices for hibernation.

When the sun warms the dusty road between the trees, a two-inch caterpillar may suddenly bustle forth. It resembles a short bottle-brush, black on the ends, brownish red in the middle. Early colonists knew it as a

129

"beare-worm." It is the woolly bear that children love. Now it marches to the middle of the path and stops, standing on ten stumpy legs while raising the front third of its body clear of the ground. From side to side the caterpillar swings its head and fore parts, as though looking for a signpost.

Down the path the insect hastens. Clearly it is the source of the colloquial expression "hurrying along like a caterpillar in the fall." At this season most kinds of caterpillars have finished feeding and have found themselves a place in which to transform into a moth or butterfly. Not so the woolly bear. It will be hungry again in the spring.

As the fur-coated creature ambles on, waves of activity rush forward along its wormlike body. First the soft, stubby legs at the rear raise and shift together. Then, as though nudged from behind, each of the four similar pairs of legs amidship lift up, move forward and come down again. Finally the three pointed pairs of legs at the front end take up the motion. A new wave now starts at the rear. The jogging gait is remarkably effective, and it is seldom interrupted even for a "look around." Rarely does this gesture lead to a sharp change in route.

On each side of its black head, the woolly bear has half a dozen minute eyes. These allow no clear vision. Yet when the caterpillar raises up and swings its head from side to side, these eyes tell the animal the way toward trees or grass or the clearing down the path. They may even help identify compass directions if the sun is bright and the sky comparatively clear.

Both crude vision and touch may warn the caterpillar that the feet of a cow or a hungry bird have come to earth close by. Usually the insect reacts by curling into a spiral, with its black and reddish bristles pointing outward in all directions. A bird may peck once or twice, then fly away, apparently discouraged. Skunks and raccoons, which relish caterpillars as food, sometimes maul a woolly bear until the brittle hairs break and fall off, leaving the soft body unprotected.

In broad daylight, under a warm autumn sun, the woolly bear is fairly safe from enemies. And with chilly nights, it develops an urge to travel. Off it goes, away from the weeds upon which it has been feeding. Down the path. Across the highway. Motorists and pedestrians may smile to see the caterpillar humping itself along. Eventually it arrives under the trees and finds a protected spot in which to spend the cold months.

Woolly bears show individuality. Some are entirely reddish brown, others are black just at the front end. Most, however, are colored in a central band and are black both fore and aft. Even then, the width of the reddish zone is variable enough to provide the basis for a popular belief. Broad colored bands on woolly bears in autumn, according to the proponents, presage a mild winter; narrow bands forecast a cold one.

All that this proportion really indicates is how early or late the weather turned chilly. Woolly bears are ready to run for shelter whenever, early in September, the first series of cool sunny days arrive. But early in the month, these caterpillars are younger, with fewer of the middle segments producing the brown hairs. Perhaps an early fall presages a long winter. At any rate, if woolly bears are more mature when they start marching to winter quarters, they do have brown hairs on more segments.

Whatever the winter, the woolly bear is ready to spend it in dormancy, curled below fallen leaves or under a board. Next spring will be time enough to return to the dozen or more favorite weeds: the plantain, the

131

grasses, the wild clovers. And although the caterpillar will sleep in its fur coat, it will emerge unmussed, immaculately groomed, every shining bristle just the right length as though freshly barbered.

Most insects keep themselves spic and span. Some spend hours daily in combing and cleaning themselves. One of these, a praying mantis now four inches long, grew to maturity in the same part of the field as the woolly bear. And although she has fine wings, she never left home. Like the caterpillar, she spent the chilly hours of darkness well down in a clump of leaves. Only after the sun warmed her thoroughly did she clamber up a stalk of goldenrod. Her first response to the dawn was merely a change in her eyes, from chocolate brown (the nighttime color) to pastel green like the rest of her body. While the woolly bear trudged along the road, she rested motionless atop the faded yellow flowers.

In the sunshine the mantis clings by her four long, slender legs to the gently waving head of goldenrod. Her front legs—the strongly muscular pair—are held in a prayerful posture just below her mouth. Whenever a fly or a wasp buzzes close to her perch, she twists her flexible neck to keep the flier straight in front of her triangular face. In this position she can observe it with both of her big compound eyes. She can decide when to snatch for her dinner, or whether to move at all.

A white butterfly flits into view and alights on a purple aster several inches away. The mantis is all attention. Her forelegs quiver slightly, as though with excitement. They are folded tightly and almost conceal the rows of spiny teeth that are so essential a part of her prey-snatching equipment.

The butterfly flips its wings. It is airborne, as lightly as a thistledown. Seemingly without effort it drifts toward the mantis and hovers over the goldenrod where she waits. Like a flash the two front legs unfold to full length. The mantis leaps toward the cabbage butterfly. Quickly she has her victim, hugging it securely in the crook of the two refolded forelegs. So firm is her spine-studded grip that the butterfly can make no move except a feeble nodding of its head. This, too, the mantis sees and stops.

Five minutes later, the butterfly's body has been consumed. Its wings drift like petals to the ground below. Then the mantis begins to clean herself. With extraordinary flexibility she contorts her forelegs and her neck to bring her mouth against every surface, licking it clean as a cat might do. Repeatedly she passes the small foot at the end of each leg through her jaws and chews it slightly. Next she turns and gives similar attention to her long middle and hind legs, working from the base of each to its tip, polishing off even the few grains of pollen that clung as a result of her sudden leap. Finally she reaches up a foreleg and draws a thread-thin feeler into her mouth, burnishing away particles invisibly small even to human eyes.

Whether the mantis lets her attention wander while cleaning her feelers is a question no one has settled. Certainly absent-mindedness is the only explanation that appeals to most human observers when they notice that each day her feelers are shorter. Today the right one may be briefer. Tomorrow the left may be still more deficient. Long before the mantis reaches the end of the feeler she is cleaning, she may suddenly clamp her jaws together and nip it through. If the autumn is mild and she survives week after week with no killing frost to end her daily bath, those feelers may become unmanageably stubby.

No longer will they reach her mouth, although she may spend ten minutes at a time attempting to claw down the brief remnants.

After every meal, and often between times, the mantis cleans herself. Otherwise she moves only seldom, and then so slowly that few potential victims take warning. But today instinct tells her something different. In response to the internal pressure of eggs ready to be laid, she hops, flies and crawls to a bush. There she clings, head downward, and begins to work the tip of her body. The valves of her egg-laying mechanism rub together. Between them a brown liquid appears, with air bubbles pressed into it to form a meringue. While continuing to build the sand-colored froth, the mantis applies it to the branch and shapes it as it dries. Then, into the growing mass of sticky foam, she slides cigar-shaped eggs. With machinelike precision she stacks one against the next and covers them with meringue. Never does she glance to see what is going on. This is the third in a series of egg masses she has built. The first one was formed just as perfectly. Each provides winter protection from sun and hungry birds for a hundred or so developing eggs.

Each autumn day, and through the nights of Indian summer in our valley, neighboring insects are placing their eggs for winter. Usually the leaves hide their activities. Meanwhile their vociferous mates—crickets, katydids, and grasshoppers—form the season's symphony orchestra. Their songs ring through the fall air, each following his own tune. Jean Henri Fabre described the music as the insects' method "of expressing the joy of living, the universal joy which every animal species celebrates after its kind."

To find delight for our senses in autumn we choose

134

particular places: the meadows and roadsides to hear the insect serenades in highest fidelity; the woodlands to revel in the wealth of color and its kaleidoscopic changes day by day; the fields again, and the orchards, for the fragrant, tasty fruits of fall. "When the frost is on the punkin and the fodder's in the shock," it is the sunny acres we choose. There the plants have been building goodness into fruits and grains all summer. Now comes their time to rest. The pendulum of the year's growth has swung from tick to tock—and stopped. It is ready for the backward stroke, when it will swing to tick again next spring. Autumn is the moment of pause.

While human eyes, ears, and noses relish the riches of autumn, smaller animals are using their own senses to complete their preparations for winter. Along the stone wall at the field border, a chipmunk dodges expertly in the tangle of woodbine. Sometimes it stops among the scarlet foliage and reaches up with mouth and forepaws for the blue berries which are held separately on branching red stems. Suddenly the chipmunk voices a series of sharp calls, the "chipping" for which it is named. Instantly, all the crickets and grasshoppers near by are silent. Instinctively they attend to the sound of an enemy in their vicinity, for chipmunks vary their diet of seeds and berries with an occasional meaty insect. Yet the same musicians pay no heed to the whistle of the groundhog standing alertly in the doorway to his underground apartment.

The groundhog is fat. His coat is sleek, and ripples as he moves. He has put on three and a half pounds since spring, and he now weighs ten. This is his winter store of food. He will not even have to reach for it while he hibernates, snug and dry, deep in his burrow. All summer

135

he has been eating well, risking the larger hawks and eagles of day, the big owls of night, to forage on a variety of plants. Occasionally he has been quick enough to catch an unwary mouse and add meat to his diet. Now even the autumn fruits seem superfluous. He is ready for a long sleep. But he cannot resist another look around, even if what he sees alarms him into an occasional whistle.

The chipmunk's fat is hidden under her mattress. Through the summer the little squirrel has been enlarging her subterranean rooms and passageways, particularly the bedroom. Now her sleeping quarters are a foot across and as much in height. The bed of fine twigs, however, is pressed against the roof with barely enough space for its owner. Hard seeds that will keep well have been slid under the matting until the combined pantry and dormitory is full. To attain her sleeping site the chipmunk has to scramble. Yet so strong is her urge to hoard that she comes home on trip after trip with her cheek pouches loaded and bulging as though she had the mumps. Now the food must be packed away in spare rooms.

The groundhog's whistle alerts the chipmunk where she sits on her diminutive haunches atop the stone wall. She raises up her three-ounce body and peers about. In her handlike forepaws she holds the remains of a locust that carelessly alighted too close. Today she has carried underground nearly an ounce of firm seeds, including a few from the succulent blue fruits of the woodbine. In spite of her feeding, she has gained no appreciable weight during the growing season. Her active body is lithe and muscular, and her hibernation will be light enough that she can feed repeatedly on her provisions while winter comes and goes. Another frost is all she needs to send her scurrying off to bed, not to emerge again until spring.

136

As the winter sets in, a silence often grips the land as though life would never reappear. Few birds are in the meadow. The last seed from the milkweed has ridden its parachute to a final destination and dropped, leaving the silk caught where goldfinches will find it for nest-lining when winter ends. Sometimes we are so engulfed in the winter silence that we begin whispering to each other.

These are the halcyon days—the time of the kingfisher in ancient legend. According to the tale, the supernatural bird flew for the solstice far out to sea and there built a floating nest in which to raise her young. Magically the halcyon quieted the weather all over the world for about two weeks, until the young ones were ready to fly on their long trip back to the haunts of men.

After the first light snow, the meadow proves to be far from deserted. Tracks of meadow mice crisscross everywhere. Running at full speed the little rodents produce paired footprints at two-inch intervals, like twinned asterisks zigzagging right and left along the route. Beside these commonest tracks of all, we often find the paired prints of weasels leaping thirteen inches at a bound, outdistancing the meadow mice with ease. In winter the predator has a real advantage, its pure-white ermine coat blending with the background entirely except for the black tip of its bushy tail. Only the snowshoe hare—white except for its black-tipped ears—is so well protected.

The hare usually puts its forefeet down side by side, and shows spread toe marks from its big back feet ❧﹡　❧﹡　❧﹦ whereas the uncamouflaged cottontail rabbit marks the snow with a finer pattern of splotchy

137

The trunk and spreading limbs of an old beech cast sprawling shadows on the winter snow. Under the snow's insulation many animals remain active.

colons in slanting italics, alternating with two hyphens ⠂⠂ ⠂⠂ ⠂⠂ ⠂⠂ . The weasel pursues these too, and we trace its leaps. Often its trail crosses or follows the intermittent series of paired colons :: :: :: between two trees, showing the way a gray squirrel traveled.

If we are lucky, we find the irregular line of round marks made by a small fox. But to see whether the claws were extended, as they are on the foot of a fox, or were retracted (as a domestic cat holds them while walking) takes real sleuthing. Both of these animals often put a rear foot down in the same snow mark the front foot just left, making one hole in the snow do for two feet—and confusing the prints of each.

138

Unpredictably, a loud report like a gunshot comes from the pond above the dam. No one is there but the muskrat, huddled beneath his mud roof, which is now frozen cement-hard. The millpond has merely acquired a new crack, into which even now the water may be welling up, to freeze and heal the gap. Or tomorrow the narrow crevasse may still be there, a trap for a skater's blade.

All too seldom do we emerge from the snugness of our hearthside into the long winter night to listen and to admire the snowy landscape. When floodlit by a moon nearly full, the snow crystals glitter and sparkle almost as brightly as the stars. It seems incredible that the brilliance at our feet comes from our own sun, now hidden from sight by the bulk of the earth, yet reflected from the distant moon. It transforms each breath we exhale into a crystal cloud, and helps us cast black shadows on the solid froth of frozen water squeaking below our feet.

A rounded lump on a low branch becomes an owl with upright tufts of feathers over the ears. We say nothing; neither does the bird. Great yellow eyes blink in our direction, singly or together. Suddenly, without a sound, the owl is airborne. Through the bushes at the edge of the meadow it banks in the manner of a stunt pilot to dodge a branch. In full moonlight the trick looks easy, but the owl achieves the same silent disappearance when light is almost lacking. Now the bird swoops low over the snow and glides with great wings spread, silent as any mouse, ready to pounce on one. No mouse appears in the bird's path, and the owl rises to a new perch in a distant tree. Still there has been no sound. We are about to move on when across the field comes the voice we have waited for—a querulous quavering in a high key, like a note on a well-played musical saw: the soft song of the screech owl.

139

Most of our friends are more interested in looking for shadows by day, particularly on the second of February. It is curious that a pagan date set aside by pre-Christian Romans should be noticed so regularly in a new era and a new world. The Romans observed the day to honor Februa, the goddess who was the mother of the god Mars and who gave her name to the month. Early Christians adopted it as Candlemas, celebrating the purification of the Virgin Mary after the birth of her Child. Country folk in the Old World looked on that date to the hibernating animals for predictions of the length of winter still to come. And when America was colonized, they transferred the legendary abilities of hedgehog and badger in northern Europe to our groundhog—whence our Groundhog Day. But the groundhog is still sound asleep in his burrow wherever he happens to be in the Oyster River valley. Neither sun nor storm will rouse him for weeks to come.

After Groundhog Day comes the harshest winter weather. These are the weeks that end the lives of deer and shrew and bird if these animals cannot find enough to eat and maintain their body temperature. It is then that the few robins that did not migrate search out the fruits of bittersweet and multiflora rose. Goldfinches showing scarcely a touch of gold hunt for ragweed thrusting through the snow, and for evening primrose whose seeds give faint reminder of butter-yellow blossoms. Grosbeaks and grouse prune buds from dormant trees. Now the bird calls in the valley are those of winter residents, including kinglets and redpolls from the subarctic. Siskins and crossbills have come south temporarily, far from their northern woodlands. Many of the chickadees and crows that winter in the valley are actually displaced far-northerners too. They replace ap-

140

parently identical birds that have moved toward the still-sunny south.

Perhaps the noisy blue jays, the owls, and the wood-peckers are the most faithful, for whom no other place is home. And every day the big pileated opens up a new galleryful of ants in a dead tree, making the forest ring with his hammering and showering fragrant wood chips upon the snow. Often the chickadees and nuthatches suspend their vigilant policing of bark for insect eggs to follow the big woodpecker and pick up any grubs he has overlooked in the fresh cavity.

Under the loose bark on a dead tree, many kinds of insects wait out the winter. Ladybird beetles are sociable at this season, and hundreds of them often hibernate in the same tree. Among them are black darkling beetles and sometimes a cricket or two.

By February we know that the sun is coming back. Dawn arrives a minute earlier every morning. The last red rim of the sun dips below the horizon two minutes later each afternoon. Slowly the ice-green band fades in the west and night comes on. Often, after the stars appear, they pale again by contrast with the great fanning arcs of white or purple, the rippling curtains of the northern lights.

It will soon be time to drive a spile into the sunny side of each tree in the sugar bush, and listen to the first sap plopping into the bucket hung below. A drop, or two, or three, each minute through the increasingly warm days; none at all during frosty nights. About a hundred and twenty thousand drops to ten gallons, to be boiled down to a quart of syrup, or a quarter pound of sugar. Thirty-nine drops to be hauled and evaporated for every one saved. It takes a lot of cordwood and tending of the fire below the pans to make a gallon of syrup. Yet if the work is to be done at all in the Oyster River valley, it must come before the spring equinox—before the maple buds pop open and summon the early honeybees. After that the syrup has a "buddy" taste.

The last snows of winter are "sugar snows," on which the minute black springtail insects leap about. They climb the trees and fall into the sap buckets, but rarely drown. They are too light in weight to break through the surface film. These strange little creatures, named from their ability to spring high in the air by suddenly straightening out the body (and not from the time of year), are among the most primitive of living insects on earth. No one knows how far into the past their ancestry extends. Certainly they were well established when the coal in the hod was still part of trees growing in a

142

The slightest breeze blows the soft fur of the alert red fox and brings scents of many kinds to help the animal in its hunting.

Carboniferous swamp three hundred million years ago, in a land where winter never came.

Every day now brings spring closer. The bright sun points energetic rays into the hard-packed snow and evaporates it, leaving rough points between the vacant channels. As the weather warms a little, snowbanks collapse to slush. Under them the water trickles. Little gurgling sounds become a song in the lesser streams, as waters from a hundred hillsides coalesce and play slapping tunes on thin vanes of ice. Farther down the valley, where a thousand hillsides have contributed their water, the river rushes headlong, tearing at its banks.

143

After a week of warmth, the roar of the cataract over the dam is almost frightening as the river plunges into the estuary and onward toward the sea.

Spring

It was as a fisherman, experienced in the out-of-doors, that Henry van Dyke remarked: "The first day of spring is one thing, and the first spring day is another. The difference between them is sometimes as great as a month." Yet many living things seem ready to ignore the vagaries of weather and keep to their innate schedule. With the equinox, the snowdrops push up from the soil. Often they melt their way through ice that lingers in the shade of evergreens. New growth appears among the cattails in the marsh. It provides food for wild geese that descend from the sky to settle on the Oyster River. It is not enough food to tempt the geese to stay, but sufficient to give them a hearty breakfast before the gaggles rise again at dawn, each goose honking as it goes.

Day and night, still other sharp chevrons of migrant flocks point north along their invisible skyway. The geese match astonishingly well the hesitant northward progress of springtime—about forty miles a day. They find open water where only a few days earlier the rivers and ponds were roofed with ice. For about a month they stay close to a single temperature—the isotherm of 35 degrees Fahrenheit—following it perhaps all the way from the coastal marshes along the Gulf of Mexico to breeding grounds near Hudson Bay. To us on the ground, noticing the rhythmic change in the season, it seems incredible that the geese should find the weather almost constant.

Gradually the calories from the sun accumulate. In the smaller streams and marshy places, a change of less than a degree in the temperature of the icy water alerts diminu-

The male tree cricket raises his flat transparent wings high over his back and moves them together to produce a trilling, bell-like call. Though female tree crickets are deaf, they approach a singing male to browse on an odorous gland he exposes when his wings are raised in the singing position.

145

tive tree frogs hibernating in the mud. The peepers awake and push their way out, where they can perch on the leafless bushes or the cold shore. The males *peep* so loudly for mates that they can be heard a mile away. By April they have told everyone it's spring. Each rivulet and marsh is fairly popping with the shrill single cries of these inch-long frogs.

Within a week or two, female peepers begin cementing their tiny eggs separately to supporting objects near the surface of little backwaters in the flooded streams. Soon thousands of them hatch into black tadpoles scarcely bigger than animated commas. Some escape being eaten, stranded, or swept downstream. Among the bottom muck they find enough microscopic nutriment to grow an inch and a third in length, and then to be transformed into air-breathing, insect-snatching peepers half that long.

Without any leader, each froglet emerges from the stream, clambers through the underbrush to the nearest tall tree, and starts up it. Adhesive pads at the tip of each toe let the peeper climb safely to sixty feet or more above the ground. There the older generations of its kind have been ever since the end of the mating season. In daylight, insects of small size settle at their peril within reach of a peeper's sticky tongue. Peepers, in turn, are endangered whenever a bluejay or other big sharp-eyed bird alights on the branch where the little frog inconspicuously crouches.

While the peepers are still laying their eggs, the toads of the Oyster River valley gather like senior citizens around the margins of all the shallow ponds. The males puff out their throats and trill in long-continued invitations to a mate. Gradually the amphibian chorus swells to its peak, its greatest variety for the year. Leopard frogs arrive and chirp explosively. Some have high-

146

pitched voices, others sound almost as guttural as a bullfrog. The combined effect is staccato and rhythmically complex, a din so loud that the shrill peeping of the little tree frogs is lost entirely.

After the herons arrive from their southern winter quarters, the frogs ordinarily become silent by day; a frog that cries out is likely to be eaten. The nocturnal chorusing of amphibians almost ceases too about the time the night herons first put in their appearance. Then we notice the pond turtles basking in the sun on half-submerged trunks of trees. While their black shells shine in the morning light as though polished, the turtles are absorbing much warmth from the sun. This increases their alertness. It speeds digestion and growth and reproduction to a degree that would be impossible for a turtle swimming through the chilly waters of the river.

Over the pond and its turtles, the kingfishers are rocketing, diving for minnows. The lily pads are at the surface again, with here and there a green flake of floating duckweed. Low over the water the swallows swoop, taking a toll of early mosquitoes and of shadflies, which are mayflies that do not wait until May to emerge. On a shrub near the stream, one phoebe calls petulantly, incessantly repeating its name. Its mate is renovating a nest under the bridge below the dam.

The old rhyme about April showers is only partly true in the Oyster River valley. Skunk cabbages along the swampy streams, pussy willows displaying their golden pollen at the wet edge of the meadow, fragrant arbutus on drier ground, and hepaticas in the deep woods, all finish flowering before May. We find them while spice-bush buds are opening, while the maples are abuzz with bees, and while scaly fiddleheads of ferns are rising from the loose forest soil by about one musical note each

Among the earliest of wildflowers are the purple-streaked cups of skunk cabbage which push up, sometimes through a late cover of snow, from swamp soil and are pollinated by early flies.

day. Already the spiders are out, prospecting their woodland hunting grounds and leaving single strands of cobweb strung from shrub to shrub. Mourning cloak butterflies settle on the bark and flash their winter-tattered wings in the sun.

After winter's white of snow and black of leafless trees, spring offers a whole spectrum to delight the senses. In the shadiest places, the red petals of wake-robin spread widely above the trio of leaves that identify the plant as a *Trillium*. Golden dandelions open beside the path—the surest gold of the whole year. Greens are everywhere, no two exactly alike. White giant stars of bloodroot

148

turn to the sky; white violets hang softly near the earth. Purple violets open, and purplish brown appears in neat stripes upon the green of upright jack-in-the-pulpits.

The heat of the sun has not yet begun to disperse the breath of spring. The air moves horizontally or stays in pockets. Sometimes we find warm ones along the crest of the meadow in the twilight after a long clear day. They remind us of just the opposite—the cold springs emerging into the warmer water where we go swimming. But mostly we are conscious of what our noses report— the sweet scent of flowers opening before the leaves reach full size, or the fragrance of wet earth.

From underground, the chipmunk that hibernated in a burrow near our back door emerges in the week when silver maple blossoms are attracting the honey-bees—the same bees that later will pollinate the apple orchards. Often the chipmunk sits up alertly with her fore paws clenched like hands against her chest, and we see that she has been nursing babies in her subterranean retreat. Her foraging supports a whole family, and keeps her busy. Not until the silver maples spin down their dry winged fruits will the chipmunk lead her youngsters into the sun and introduce them to the delicacies on the porch. By then the first brood of young song sparrows will have left the nest. The robins and wrens will be dashing about from dawn to dusk, flying a shuttle service with worms and insects of gradually increasing size to fit the growing hungry mouths.

Two-thirds of the way through the greening month of May is the time to visit the sunny apple orchards and listen to the bees. In each tree their wings produce a companionable humming that is almost as loud there as the sound of the motor from a light airplane overhead. The pilot sees each orchard only as a great rectangle in

The graceful spirals in fern fiddleheads, as they unroll in springtime, add dignity and delight to the woodlands. The soft green of fern fronds has a timeless quality that has continued on the forest floor since the Coal Ages.

pinkish white, fitting the contours of the land. We look up under the apple trees and distinguish (as he cannot from an altitude of a few thousand feet) the individual blossoms and the bees that are darting, hovering, or creeping among them. In the transformation of the energy of sunlight into apples, the visit of individual bee to individual flower is an essential step.

When we think about it, we realize that time has favored apple trees and other plants that invest some of their raw materials and sun-derived energy in floral advertising—in petals and scent—by which a bee can be guided to patronize the flower. By brushing past the stamens dusty with pollen and the pistil to which pollen grains adhere so easily, the bee is able to reach a drop of moisture sweetened with energy-rich sugar. The sugar water, secreted as nectar in the bottom of the blossom, is a fee paid by the plant to its pollinator.

The bees in the apple orchard claim a good deal of the pollen too. At frequent intervals each bee uses special combs and brushes on her legs to clean the golden particles from her body. Often she hovers over a flower while working her legs to transfer the pollen. She wets it with nectar or with regurgitated honey brought from the hive, and packs it into masses resembling saddle-bags. Bees with well-filled pollen baskets soon head for home. In the hive the pollen is transferred to cells around the brood comb. Younger sisters work the material into "bee bread" or feed upon it, preparatory to secreting special food for immature bees.

The pollen taken by the bees is actually an investment the flowering plants make toward keeping honeybees in existence. It is another contribution toward the partnership of flower and bee. To develop properly, a honeybee requires an amount of proteins, minerals, and vitamins
151

equivalent to a hundred loads of pollen, representing almost a hundred thousand visits to separate flowers. A flower, however, needs only a few pollen grains carried to the right place to make the partnership worth while.

Under wild conditions, each seed that develops after pollination is like a lottery ticket—a slim chance that the parent will win. The prize is a place in posterity, by reproducing another tree like, although not identical with, itself. Each small brown seed contains an embryonic apple tree with two thick white leaves, already loaded with food materials. Upon this little hoard, supplied by the parent tree, the seedling depends for a few weeks while raising new green leaves toward the sun.

Apple seedlings stand a good chance of germinating elsewhere in the valley, far from the parent tree. Those of pine, by contrast, seldom travel far. When a white pine spreads open its downturned cones in spring, it lets the breeze carry its winged naked seeds to fend for themselves. But an apple tree encloses each dozen seeds in a pulpy fruit. The sweet pulp is a further gamble, a bribe for an animal, such as a raccoon, an opossum, or a deer, that enjoys windfalls. Often the animal will carry the enclosed seeds to some distant place and there discard them after eating the fruit. Only through having a great many seeds transported by animals is one of them likely to be ready to germinate when all the conditions are right for it to survive to maturity and the production of more apple seeds.

Most apple trees produce more flowers in alternate springs. This lets us anticipate more apples in years of abundant flowers. Orchardists say that in each apple the tree stores approximately the amount of energy captured by eighteen square feet of apple leaves in an hour of summer sunlight, when the roots have plenty of water.

Through most of the day, the nighthawk rests motionless. Between eyelids that almost meet in a horizontal slit, the bird watches for danger.

It is equivalent to three heaping teaspoonfuls of sugar. To us, this seems a lot to risk on transportation for a few seeds. But it is a clear admission that no apple tree in the valley lives to itself. It relies on its neighbors.

The vitalizing sunshine and refreshing rains of springtime mean more than bees in flowers and frogs in ponds, more than apples and grains to come. They are invitations to appreciate the life of the valley that is surging forward as at no other time of year. We can respond with countless different visits to our plant and animal neighbors in the orchards, the fields, the water world, and the woodlands. We may reassure ourselves that both bluebirds of a pair are cleaning the apple tree of caterpillars and other insects, carrying them to their young. The groundhog in the orchard is in good voice, and as curious as ever. Through fields starry with white daisies we can amble to the dam. If the time and tide are right,

153

a shoal of alewives will be heading toward the barrier, their dorsal fins breaking through the rushing water.

After the sun is high, the shores of the estuary call. There horseshoe crabs are mating in a ritual they have followed for half a billion years. In the coolness of the woods, the thrushes are voicing their thrilling melodies. Each evening the great cecropia moths and the pale lunas emerge from these same woods to flit gracefully below the street lamps, like ballet dancers under the spotlight on a darkened stage. Beyond the illumination, down where the Oyster River flows quietly past the blackness of the forest and the damp of the marsh, fireflies once more punctuate the night with the dots and dashes that are the cold sparks of their silent code.

On the ground below, where only a few hours earlier the ferns and fallen logs reflected the last daylight, juvenile fireflies—the glowworms—dine on snails. Wherever they parade go bright pinpricks of yellow or green. Tree frogs see these lights too, and sometimes make a meal of the worms. Once a steady glow led us to the bole of a big beech, on which a two-inch frog clung with sticky toes. It had swallowed so many glowworms and fireflies that light from the dying insects in its distended stomach shone through its body wall and faintly illuminated the bark as well.

The rhythm of life quickens in springtime as at no other season. Before the sun becomes too hot and the moisture scanty, every living thing seems hurrying to reproduce, to feed its young, to get the most out of the long days. Everywhere the valley beckons us at once, as though inviting enjoyment of this brief repetition of the springs from previous years—this fleeting sample we must capture now or wait three seasons to meet again.

154

Catastrophe

At least once each year, it seems, we discover in the Oyster River valley a great tree that has recently been struck by lightning. At the base of the shattered trunk, limbs as thick as a man's body lie strewn about. The tree has literally exploded, blown apart by the irresistible force of water abruptly turned to steam by the rush of electrical energy through the bark and wood. A few of these trees recover. They heal over the broad scars and reach anew for the sky with branches that invite lightning to strike again.

Where the struck tree stands alone, as many a hickory or a pine does today along the border of a field or among outcropping rocks too extensive to blast loose, the catastrophe affects chiefly the one mature plant. Any birds perching or nesting on it may be electrocuted. But when a giant tree in a close-set forest is ripped by the sudden surge of electricity from the sky to the ground,

155

the heavy fragments from its downfall are likely to break and crush many of its neighbors. One stroke of lightning can open a surprisingly big hole in a forest, letting sunlight reach the ground among the fallen pieces. In a split second it delivers a wealth of new materials to the agents of decay. Simultaneously it sounds the starting signal for a fierce race among seedlings, each of which struggles to become heir to the sunlight that was used by the riven tree.

Although we may regard with awe and respect the tall tree that recovers from one lightning bolt only to be struck again, it often remains a menace to the wild community. Usually it contains a great mass of dry dead wood which a second surge of electricity can set afire. Even though rains may wet the surface and quench the flame, its heartwood may continue to glow as a tall hidden ember. After the water has drained away, a wind can fan this to the ignition point. Most forest fires that begin naturally start from a partly dead tree that has been struck a second time. Each year in the conterminous United States, about twenty thousand fires of this kind severely damage areas totaling more than Delaware and Rhode Island together. Almost any large stand of trees is vulnerable, although with modern fire-fighting equipment the average size of the area burned has been reduced to about a twentieth of a square mile.

Not for nearly four decades has this kind of disaster struck the Oyster River valley. But the scars of one are still obvious to the south of the estuary, where a furious blaze left only the charred skeletons of the biggest trees. Not a single stump survived to send up new stems from the roots. No tree seed withstood the intense heat. Even the topsoil was first seared, and then poisoned with chemicals from the ashes. Until rains leached away the

156

soluble material, new seeds brought by wind and birds could gain no roothold. Animals that wandered into the burned tract found nothing to eat.

The fire itself came on March 29, at the beginning of a spring that was extraordinarily dry. It heated a day already unseasonably hot, and added to the wind its own powerful convection vortex of inrushing air. Thousands of board feet of pine that had been cut and stacked during the previous months went up in flames, along with the slash the woodsmen had left among the stumps.

No human lives were lost, but no count was made of wild animals that perished. From similar catastrophes beyond the valley, we can visualize some of the frantic creatures fleeing from the fire. Probably a good many deer escaped by running, even though they probably paused at intervals as though transfixed by the mysterious crackling lights, the billowing smoke, the ugly roar. Foxes too would be likely to save themselves. But any porcupines, being too slow and ill-adapted to get away, must have been cooked on the spot. Snowshoe hares, already in the brown summer pelage, are almost certain to have dashed at top speed to the limits of familiar territory, and then dashed back through the flames with coats afire, rather than leave the woods of home. A few squirrels may have traveled from tree to tree faster than the flames advanced. Others probably suffocated with their young, and vanished when the den tree became another torch in the general conflagration.

We wonder how many birds flew off unhurt, and how many returned to hunt through the smoke for insects flying aimlessly about. Elsewhere we have seen blackbirds streak for any rising cloud of smoke from a burning marsh, to take advantage of grasshoppers fleeing from disaster among the flaming vegetation. Where the road wound through the fire-struck area of the Oyster River valley, many creatures must have taken refuge in the stone walls or in roadside burrows, only to die there. Chipmunks, garter snakes, toads, wasps with paper nests among the stones, and perhaps a few groundhogs would have relied upon this ordinarily adequate protection.

After a year or two of rains had sweetened the impoverished remains of the forest soil, it became hospitable to silk-tufted seeds of fireweed. They could have come from many miles away. Some germinated and grew into tall weeds with handsome spikes of magenta flowers. From these still more plumed seeds developed, completing the quick colonization of the burned tract. Stronger winds brought the winged seeds of gray birch into the midst of the fireweeds. These seedlings too grew rapidly, and a miniature forest of slender trees rose high enough to provide perches for birds. The birds left droppings with living seeds of blackberry, wild raspberry, and rose; from these, brambles spread. On the rim of one upright hollow stump ten feet high, an unknown bird that had feasted on mountain ash fruits provided a memorial of its visit. Into the cavity it dropped some fertilizer-covered seeds. One of them grew into a mountain ash tree now twenty feet high and nearly six inches in diameter. It rises straight from the center of the old burned stump.

In spring the tangles of young birches are full of the color of darting birds. The many kinds of warblers especially find these trees a fine hunting ground for insects. But by early summer, the wasps that the birds did not catch have laid eggs on a large sampling of the birch foliage. From each egg a tiny flattened maggot has emerged to burrow into the thin triangular leaf, eating out the green tissue and leaving an unsightly brown

158

blister. The birches appear diseased, unthrifty, and incapable of competing with other trees. In their spotty shade the white pines are already beginning to rise. Birches are "nurse trees" to pines. But when the pine is grown, the birches die. Gradually the evergreens shade all of the sun-loving plants out of existence, and make a place for those that thrive in shade.

The forest that burned in the Oyster River valley was a mixed stand of pine and hardwoods, whose floor regularly became a garden of pink ladyslipper orchids about the time the whippoorwills laid their mottled eggs upon the fallen leaves. The orchids vanished utterly in the fire. But now, in a few places where pines and some hardwoods have grown tall again and the soil is thickening under the duff, ladyslippers have once more appeared. Have thrushes and other forest birds brought the tiny seeds upon their feet? A living community is so knit together that we tend to see the whole and overlook the degree to which each life depends upon others, especially when the others are of unlike kind.

A quick fire sweeping over the ground in a pine forest from time to time may actually help the trees keep ready to reproduce themselves. The fire maintains a suitable seed bed between the tall trunks, for so long as the fallen needles remain dry and not too deep, a white pine can start seedlings in its own shade. An occasional ground fire will kill the seedlings, but clear away the pine duff and keep it from accumulating. Each year a new generation of seedlings will rise, though later they die. They are preparing for the time when a mature tree grows senile, is riddled by beetles, converted into nurseries by carpenter ants, and excavated by woodpeckers. As soon as the old tree dies, young trees can reach upward and compete for the light their elder no longer captures.

159

Tall pines in dense forests are well protected from ground fires. Their thick bark insulates the vital tissues, while their habit of self-pruning—dropping off all branches that are too shaded to bear green needles—takes away the dry dead wood a fire might use like the rungs of a ladder to rise to the living crowns. However, if no fire sweeps through for several decades, the needles and branches accumulating upon the ground decompose into an acid soil which holds more moisture than a pine seedling can tolerate. Then the slow-growing hardwood seeds gain a roothold. When the old pines die, a deciduous forest replaces the evergreen one.

An occasional fire helps some of the spruces too, by scorching their fallen cones and springing them open, freeing the winged seeds within. So well adapted to tolerating sporadic disasters by fire have these trees become that they can no longer do without the blistering heat. Whereas a felled forest of such spruces may be replaced by other kinds of woody plants, a burned one that is not too severely devastated is able to rise like the phoenix from its own ashes.

The ground fire that is beneficial to a pine or spruce forest generally brings disaster to a mixed stand of hemlock and beech. The resinous needles that remain green on low branches of the hemlocks catch fire. The heat alone may be enough to kill the tender leaves of beech, or to cook the vital tissues under the thin gray bark. This difference lets us reconstruct a little of the past history in the woodlands wherever we encounter a parklike stand of hemlock and beech. Usually the area proves to be an island of unburned land, protected by a loop of the river or by swampy tracts from ground fires in the surrounding strongholds of pine and sugar maple.

Curiously, the one tree in all the valley that seems most exposed to ground fires, as well as to lightning, is a giant hemlock atop Beech Hill. Why it has not been burned in well over a century of life, or struck during an electrical storm, or cut by sawyers for tanbark and building material, we cannot imagine. Of all the trees, that one seems most liable to catastrophe.

The big hemlock withstood the disastrous hurricane of 1938, and the three others that have roared through our valley in the past decades. Each time the winds have battered the leaves to a pulp, torn apart great trees limb by limb, and flung down others in one general direction as though they were jackstraws. The thick roots snapped off and heaved out of the earth as the boles went crashing against neighboring trees or to the ground. Each time the hurricane has come somewhere around the autumn equinox. Each time it has driven the land animals, half drowned in the down-sluicing rain, to whatever shelter they could find among the stricken plants. It has swept oceanic birds such as murres and petrels far inland—and, probably, land birds to their doom far out to sea.

After the gusty gales have ceased and the sun brightens the soggy ravaged wake of the frightful storm, the birds and bees and squirrels and deer all emerge to rebuild their lives. At first they seem dazed, for so many of their landmarks have toppled, so many of their customary routes been blocked by blowdowns. Any disturbance appears to paralyze them, because habit no longer can take them swiftly to safety. Until they learn new pathways through the meaningless tangle, they are lost on the very spot where home used to be.

The calamity to the forest soon turns into a bonanza

for animals and for the lesser kinds of plants. The fallen trunks afford countless places of concealment, and give openings for the light to reach the seedlings on the ground below. Fungi and wood-boring insects multiply at an amazing pace in the defenseless wood. Insect-eating birds, tree frogs, and salamanders cannot keep up with the food supply. All year the woodpeckers hammer away. Fragments of bark and chips of wood cascade to the ground, providing there a multitude of damp, dark hideaways for insects and worms. White-footed mice and voracious shrews feast in these places. Occasionally they too are discovered by a skunk or a fox or a bear pawing through the debris for anything resembling meat.

In a few years the wood-boring insects and fungi emerging from the dead trees may begin making real inroads upon healthy living timber. With so many invaders cutting through the bark or sliding slender fungal filaments into every crevice, even the most vigorous tree is taxed to repel all its attackers simultaneously. Weaker trees are overwhelmed, and soon contribute new hordes of beetles and fungus spores, which intensify still more the attack on all survivors.

In the Oyster River valley, winters are cold enough to enforce the equivalent of a temporary truce in this battle between the trees and their attackers. Only the warm-blooded birds and mammals with a taste for insects continue work that benefits the trees. By spring, the number of beetles surviving is significantly less. With warm weather, however, these creatures once more have the advantage: they reproduce much more rapidly than any animal with fur or feathers. So long as food continues to be abundant, only a few insects need to survive in order to repopulate a woodland.

As the insects and lesser decomposers in the forest

pulverize the wood and degrade it chemically into materials containing less chemical energy and a higher content of minerals, the stricken giants of the forest melt into the soil. Their substance rises again in the vigorous young saplings that compete for the sunlight above. With time the scars of the hurricane disappear.

Winter can bring catastrophes that are more predictable than hurricanes. Sleet storms put a glistening coat of ice on tree limbs. Wet snow weights them down. Branches snap. Or the whole trunk of a tree splits wide apart. Only the birches are supple enough to bow their loaded crowns all the way to the ground, forming arches clad in gray or white bark. Many of them never straighten out fully afterward.

When we watch through our windowpanes as a blizzard brings wet snow or freezing rain, we see sparrows perched motionless with feathers fluffed out until the bird becomes an almost perfect ball, with the tail the only extended part. We wonder then about W. H. Hudson's poetic description of a bird's death, in which he declared that the feathered creature felt no apprehension and "was never miserable." How else does a bird show its misery in the bitter wind, the driving rain, the sticky snow, than by shutting its eyes and shielding its feet as best it can? So long as its feathers keep it dry and its internal store of food suffices as fuel to make good all losses of heat to the winter storm, the bird may be safe. So may a squirrel be, where it clings, head up, to the lee side of a tree trunk. But as we look about our valley on February 20, just after another six-inch fall of snow, we know that one gray squirrel is still clinging to a tall sugar maple high above the ground, at the spot where it died during a sleet storm many weeks ago.

Even if a bird or squirrel is able to keep from freezing

163

to its support and to avoid the full force of the blizzard, after the storm it faces a grim white world in which most food is buried deeply or hidden under a glaze of ice. The tree sparrows that choose seeds when they can find them in winter suddenly act like chickadees, probing the bark for insect eggs at a frantic pace that reveals their hunger. Grosbeaks and robins that failed to migrate now converge on the rose tangles and rip off the small hard hips with relish. Goldfinches and purple finches investigate the birches and elms for soft buds they can pick apart.

Deep snow slows the progress of four-footed creatures, but does not stop them. Deer are more vulnerable at this season, and in addition they have difficulty reaching buds and tender twigs as food. Many smaller mammals seem able to ignore the storms. While the February blizzard was at its worst, male skunks continued their winter rounds, finding females in their dens. Those that succeeded in the search will become fathers the second week of April, although they will not join the family until July, when the youngsters are old enough to be taught the arts of hunting. Moles under the snow, raccoons above it, minks and otters along the river, muskrats in the marsh, flying squirrels in tree holes, all risk catastrophe in midwinter to insure the arrival of new generations when the winter's grip relaxes. Their persistence and speed outstrip the Persian messengers so highly praised by Herodotus, instinctively sustaining the tradition inscribed in 1913 on a post-office door: "Neither snow, nor rain, nor heat, nor gloom of night, stays these couriers from the swift completion of their appointed rounds."

Most catastrophes are local, and serve to set back the normal succession of living things to an earlier stage. They destroy the aged, the infirm, the conservative; they upset the status quo. They make places for new lives, for a fresh testing of adaptations among the competitors for space and energy. They help evolution to progress another little step. The plants and animals today are the survivors, and the descendants of survivors, from countless catastrophes in the past. They are what they are more as a result of this long succession of calamities than of the good times that intervened between one disaster and the next.

Only from man's point of view is a toppled tree or a dead squirrel wasted. The soil and the air in which all land creatures have their origin are composed of the identical atoms that made up the molecules of prehistoric life. Endlessly the same building blocks are fitted together and then torn down again. Each edifice is different: the deer from the dinosaur, the pine of today from the magnolia of ten million years ago.

We can only suppose that it makes no difference to a carbon atom whether it is in the protoplasm of a birch tree or of a goldfinch, in a bit of limestone, or in the carbon dioxide carried by the breeze. It makes no difference to the Oyster River valley whether it is smothered under ice, or clad in forests, or reduced by burning to organic matter in the topsoil. Only man is conscious of what might have been, or reads the records of what went before and mourns its passing. For his living neighbors it is enough that after winter comes the spring, after bad times come the good. By comparison with the long sweep of life upon the earth, most catastrophes are so transitory as to be inconsequential. Yet each of them slightly alters the constitution of the community that rebuilds itself, and has its part in shaping what the future holds in store.

165

The Mark of Man

Just as a bucket of ocean water loses something when it is separated from the restless sea, so too our valley retains its vitality only so long as it is part of the rest of the world. The comings and goings of living things that know few lasting boundaries are essential to the changing landscape. But of all the creatures that have entered the New World, none has done so much to bring about change as men from Europe. They have endowed each hill and point of land in our valley with some special lore. They continue to provide its intimate color and to extend its brief tradition.

It is easy to identify ourselves with the pioneers and to relish their exploits. We feel a kinship with Darby Field, the inquisitive settler who got the first bird's-eye view over this part of our country and was the first to scale a major mountain in North America. From shipboard along the Atlantic Coast he had glimpsed a series of snow-clad peaks lying inland and north of the tip of Oyster River Point, where the estuary opens into Great Bay. These peaks, however, were invisible from the waterways he traveled between the isolated communities recently hewed from the dense forest.

One arm of Great Bay led toward the mountains. It seems likely that Darby Field followed this arm into the Salmon River, along the present boundary between New Hampshire and Maine. At its headwaters, forty-five miles of virgin forest still separated him from the Presidential Range. Yet in 1642 he traveled from the valley and reached his goal, climbing Mount Washington to its summit. To accomplish this, he braved hostile Indians and also the wrath of their Great Spirit, for his superstitious guides were sure that their god would destroy this impudent white man who was determined to assault the sacred heights.

In Darby Field's day, men had already begun to alter the direction in which the Oyster River valley would develop. Around 1631, at the westernmost point in Great Bay to which a sturdy ocean-going ship could pass—Durham Landing, just below the final rocky falls of the river—a wooden dam was built. It flooded one long reach of the valley as no beaver dam had ever done. It also supplied water for a combined saw mill and grist mill. Great logs for the mill floated down the waterway above the dam, and were hauled up a ramp to the saw. In winter the sawyer and the miller, who occupied a two-family house near their work, cut ice from the millpond (they called it a "freshet") and buried the blocks in sawdust, producing a refrigerator in which fish

167

and meat would stay fresh for weeks even in midsummer.

The tallest, straightest, stoutest trees became masts for ships built in Europe or for those known as "gundalows," which were built on the shore opposite Durham Landing. A gundalow's sail was lateen-rigged, giving the vessel a resemblance to the Arab dhows on the Mediterranean and along the coasts of Africa. Less valuable trees became logs for small cabins, or for the thick walls of fortified houses ("garrisons"). Almost half of the homes in the Oyster River valley were garrisons from which Indians could be driven off. Despite these precautions, massacres continued as late as 1794—four years after the first census of white settlers in the Colonies was made.

By far the greatest number of trees went into fuel with which to keep living quarters warm through the cold months. Additional blocks of forest vanished in flames, as the soil was cleared to make space for crops. Gradually the valley became checkered with rolling farm land from which rose great outcropping ledges of granite. Loose boulders were hauled to build long lines of stone walls reputed to be "sheep high, bull strong, and pig tight."

As the forests diminished, few noticed that rivulets from melting snow and summer rains were carrying away the soil previously held by the roots of trees. Above the dam at Oyster River Falls, the long reach of clear water filled with dark mud. Cattails took root, and alders interlaced their shrubby branches. Below the dam, more sediments settled. They came too from all the other rivers pouring into Great Bay. Within two centuries after the first dam was built at the falls of the Oyster River, ocean-going vessels began sticking in mudflats except at extreme high tide as they traveled to Durham Landing.

168

The shipbuilders now had to wait until the tide in Great Bay was full before launching the keelless gundalow hulls they crafted.

Still the village grew. Opposite the combined saw and grist mill, a tannery was built. Soon the tanner added a monument works to his establishment, where he could cut granite tombstones for pioneers who died and boundary markers for the property of those who survived. Later, this same mill grew famous as the place for taking surplus apples to in the fall, to have them converted into cider and apple butter, which would keep all winter long. After the construction of roads, a blacksmith shop and livery stable opened. Horsemen grew used to reining up while a load of long straight poles was hauled toward the wharf below the dam. Many of these masts, destined for the Royal Navy of Charles I, were cut within musket range of Spruce Hole, along a forest trail that is still known as the Mast Road.

Every spring the people of the village wondered whether the dam would hold under the violent assault of floods on the previously peaceful river. Every summer the same people had to count on unpredictable rains to keep the millpond full enough to give power for the cider mill. The saw mill closed for want of logs to cut. The grist mill ran only a few hours at intervals of a week or more.

As the soil grew thinner, rockier, and less productive, many a farmer gave up and moved out—traveling westward along the new roads. Sometimes a neighbor used the cleared land for pasturing his livestock. Oftener it grew up in blackberries and spiraea bushes, wild rose and staghorn sumac, field birch and poplar. Slowly the pines and oaks closed in, bringing back the forest. It hid the long stone walls so laboriously constructed. It hid

169

the cellar holes and the abandoned wells, into which had gone so much hope and care.

This pattern of man-made changes in the little valley of the Oyster River is familiar all over the East. Only the dates for each locality differ slightly. We can walk from the here and now—our particular place and time— into a sort of universal early America merely by going the short distance to the edge of the river and sitting a while on a big rock from which we can watch in both directions. Only fifty years ago, residents of an earlier generation had a little rustic summerhouse bolted to this vantage point. At night they held parties in the frame mansion at the top of the hill, and guided their guests along the path to the summerhouse on the big rock by means of Japanese lanterns. Three hundred years ago, only the Indians knew the course the water followed— and they had no lamps to guide their feet in darkness. Now the summerhouse, the lanterns, and the Indians are gone.

Above the backwaters of the dam, the stream passes through a riffle with large moss-covered stones the Indians might have used as we do, in crossing to the other side. We balance, and jump, and are into the fringing alders. Pressing up the bank, we emerge into a bit of second- or third-growth woodland deep in fallen cones of hemlock and leather-brown leaves of beech. Gazing down at the dark water below the crossing place, it is easy to imagine how the countryside was when oaks now more than a century old were sprouting from the acorn.

Yet it is important to realize what changes have altered the valley since the Indians walked its trails. One of the most conspicuous is a swath through the forest past Beech Hill, cut and patrolled by people from the power company. Chemical sprays keep the oaks and birches from coming back. Most of the other alterations are the products of ax and saw, of dynamite stick and bulldozer, of cement mixer and paving machine. These devices have leveled most of the woodlands as well as many of the smaller hills. They have dammed some of the valley and filled various low places. Usually they have buried the rich forest soil, or hurried it as silt down the streams in flood time. They seem to have devastated the land much as did the great glaciers, although on a smaller scale. We wonder how important they actually are in the evolution of living things in the valley.

We chose this area after looking at a thousand others, as a place in which to make our home. The Indian, in most instances, was born, did his hunting, and died within a tract smaller than we may drive over in our car before lunch. We think of the Oyster River valley as a place of many pleasures but few extremes—a quiet, self-contained, thoroughly New England habitat. The Indian must have thought of it in the same way, for he named the river the Shankhassick, and followed its trails to the oyster beds along the estuary.

The Indians came and went over the low boundary hills, but left the valley largely as they found it. They slipped between the tall trees of the mature forest, avoiding the fallen logs except where a solid barkless one bridged a small gully.

When the Great Spirit was willing, an alert Indian might meet a deer and fell it, whatever the season, with a well-placed arrow. Its body meant a feast of venison, soft skin for moccasins and leather pouches, a bladder for carrying water, and bits of bone from which symmetrical arrow points could be carved on a stormy day. Seeing a deer suggests few of these things to us, partly because our stomachs are filled more often.

171

The deer trails the Indians followed before our time were used by black bears too. In the Indian's eyes, a small bear was next best to a deer. Its meat was good; its fat had many uses; and its long-haired hide could serve as a rug or a blanket for use in winter, if it was not too heavy to carry home. But its bones were hard to crack, and other parts of the bear had less value to an Indian than the corresponding pieces of a deer.

With luck, an Indian following the irregular bends of the descending river might surprise a beaver, make a meal from its flesh, and then add its soft pelt to the trophies already tied to his deerskin belt. Venison, bear, goose, beaver, squirrel—the Indian accepted each kind of meat gratefully. By eating its flesh, he believed that he took into his own body the strength and alertness of the wild creature itself. So many of the characteristics of animals were abilities he admired from patient observation, that he deliberately sought their flesh as food and thus gave his diet variety. In a sense, self-improvement was one reason for hunting through the Oyster River valley every few moons.

We go oftener, but with different motives. Our pleasures are chiefly esthetic, rarely gastronomic—contemplative rather than utilitarian. We might still meet a bear, for its kind are around. One that visited the Oyster River valley during the past decade made a nuisance of itself. For nearly a week it knocked over a beehive or two every night, and got to the honey despite the stings of sleepy bees. Then, perhaps unnerved by flashing lights, loud noises, and angry beekeepers, the bear left.

No longer is there any chance that we might come face to face with an Indian, or that our path would take us into an acre of virgin forest left standing. Only the

172

ghosts of Indians, of giant trees, of passenger pigeons and beaver families parade before us as we try to think back to an earlier scene in this selfsame place.

Which of the features in the present landscape would be visible a century hence, were our own ghosts to revisit the Oyster River valley? Would there still be orchards and beehives, and perhaps bears to raid them in the night? How the ponds and the river, the meadows and forests will fare if viewed "only" as esthetic assets, paying little tax to the town, depends upon the beliefs of the men who can control their fate.

The pace of change grows ever swifter. Automobiles now speed from all directions toward the White Mountains, that were explored at real risk three centuries ago by Darby Field. The hotel atop Mount Washington has celebrated a hundred years' use of the "carriage road" to the summit. But the wild creatures in the rising forests and flowing streams of every valley seem to ignore the rumble of trucks, the roar of bulldozers, and the thunder of jet aircraft overhead. Just as life has done for uncounted millions of years, it retains its resiliency. It waited out the Ice Ages, and waits now for man to rediscover how to share the earth.

Epilogue

Since our chapters were first written, the valley has changed in ways that repeat the past and portend the future.

Beech Hill has again lost its forest cover. Woodsmen felled and hauled away every tree that would yield a board or a bolt for someone's fireplace. The giant hemlock is gone. A sawcut through the annual rings at its base showed its age to be 173 years. For a few seasons, it was easy to visit the big boulder with its deep scratches from millenia ago. (A geologist friend assures us that those grooves correspond to the direction of ice movement only by chance. The boulder is a huge erratic left by the melting ice, and the whole of Beech Hill is a drumlin of debris with no rigid rocky core.) Now tree saplings are rising again, concealing such ancient history.

A female mute swan—the royal bird of Britain and a native of Europe from Poland to the delta of the Danube—settled like a gift from the sky on the mill pond and accepted the welcome proffered by the townspeople. When she tried to wait out a New England winter, despite a roof of ice thickening above the water, we knew she needed help. She spent one snow season alone at the University and a second in the company of a male brought as a potential mate from a wild flock in Rhode Island. Now free-flying, these magnificent white birds follow a schedule of their own, like the famous swallows of San Juan Capistrano. In winter the swans fly eastward to coastal waters where tidal currents keep ice from forming over a supply of wild foods. In March, as regularly as Town Meeting, the pair return to reassert their claim to the mill pond and nearby waters in Durham. No cultural development has ever sustained town interest as has this pair of swans. They tend a nest each spring where swans never lived before. Because of the swans, smaller water birds come in greater

174

numbers to the mill pond. Its shining waters focus attention on a beauty spot that reflects enjoyment of wildlife as consistently as the water reflects the sky.

Recently this reflection faded. After the swans, the mallards, and the wood ducks raised their annual families, workmen arrived to repair the old dam on the river to install a new fish ladder. They opened wide the rusty gates at the dam for the first time in many years. The mill pond and its backwaters drained completely in less than two days, allowing access to the foundations of the dam. But through the opened gates swept countless fishes, turtles, immature insects, and other inconspicuous life—everything loose upon which the denizens of the pond had depended for food. Below the dam these creatures met death in the intolerable salt water of the estuary.

Only a trickle of Oyster River traced the bottom of the stream through the former pond. Across it in two places the resident beavers attempted to salvage their world with new dams. But the stream flow was too scant, the channel at their dam sites too open for them to succeed. The beavers quickly moved elsewhere, as did the muskrats, otters, swans, ducks, and herons. Freshwater mussels in unbelievable numbers remained stranded. Their bivalved shells gaped on the drying mud of the pond and river bottom. Dozens of shore birds from the Atlantic coast arrived and stalked about, eating what they could of mussel flesh and small creatures hiding shallowly in the mud itself. The native animals of the pond and its backwaters perished, as did water lilies and other aquatic plants that could not tolerate the dry air and hot sun week after week. It seemed incredible to us that elected officials and wildlife agencies should knowingly sacrifice so many lives.

All of us on shore marveled to see how little water the pond had held. Silt filled its weedy shallows. A few people recognized the accumulation as topsoil from bared forest land higher in the valley, and sand from various construction sites upstream. The dam gates were closed again six weeks later. In a few days, aided by a thundershower, the pond refilled with water, if not with life. Three years afterward, large dead remains of water lilies were still rising from the bottom, to float slowly to the dam. The pond had not yet fully regained its hospitality to aquatic life.

The sources of silt increased abruptly again, postponing once more Nature's adjustments toward former ways, toward renewing the Oyster River valley. Our favorite meadow slope along one side of the pond became raw earth as bulldozers pushed the goldenrods and asters, the meadow mice, the nests of birds and bumblebees into high piles as "valuable topsoil." This converted the area into foundation holes and level land, where few American plants or animals would be welcome. These original tenants of our valley were squeezed out. The former meadow now shelters various introduced tame grasses and shrubbery and people, each in an assigned and tended place. But even these changes may be modified by care to incorporate, rather than to destroy, the gifts of Nature.

The sloping pasture between the pond and the white church on the hill has also vanished. No longer can a walker by the water glance up to see bluebirds and bobolinks and meadowlarks flitting to feed among the weeds, or to notice a cow or two grazing in circles, each tethered to a stake driven into the pasture soil. The cows are gone, and the cow barn is transformed into an apartment house. Where purple martins used to congregate, energized by eating countless mosquitoes, a paved road leads automobiles to parking spaces.

The shallowing of the mill pond with silt made itself evident when finally the fish ladder was activated. The season seemed perfect for fishes to leap weir after weir, up steps of flowing water from the estuary to the pond. Smelts, shad, alewives, and salmon arrived as expected. Yet neither the pond nor the Oyster River could supply

176

enough water for the fish ladder without draining the system disastrously. The ladder had to be closed down in less than two days. The ecological history of the valley progresses faster than we notice and influences the benefits from new amenities as well as old.

These changes so short a distance beyond our doorstep differ only in the fine details from those we observe elsewhere. Always, it seems, something lurks beyond human plans to interfere with simple success. In the next river basin, just beyond our boundary hills, the flow of water was sufficient to keep an older fish ladder operating. But it too had been closed at the height of the spawning run, because sea lampreys took up positions at each weir and seized upon the full-grown fishes as they ascended the ladder in single file.

Henry David Thoreau summed up our complex world neatly in his records of a week on the Concord and Merrimack rivers: "By one bait or another, Nature allures inhabitants into all her recesses." Long before Thoreau, the Reverend Gilbert White of Selbourne noted the nearly countless knots in the web of life when he declared that "all nature is so full that the district produces the greatest variety, which is the most examined."

Our own delights arise from sharing Thoreau's "singular yearning toward all wildness," and an almost impartial inquisitiveness about the natural world. We aspire to Gilbert White's patience in seeking to understand and appreciate our nonhuman neighbors. Repeatedly we feel surprise that so many of them conduct their lives in almost identical ways all across the north temperate zone, sometimes far beyond it and often in close proximity to people with different cultures.

In one way, however, the citizens of the Oyster River valley distinguished themselves as particularly sensitive to the commonplace features of native America. A few years ago they rallied together and voted against development of an industrial complex through conversion of a

177

tract of regrown forest and scattered farms. They rejected an oil refinery in their midst, intended to serve New England and to be connected by pipeline over land and water to an unloading facility for supertankers miles out to sea. Our neighbors (and we are proud of them) decided that unexploited land offered more toward happiness than all the tempting payments or the promised opportunities for employment. A whole nation applauded this response to a tantalizing tradeoff, and respected the respondents who so appreciate living space.

We hope this too portends decisions to be made elsewhere, to lessen the impact of mankind pitted against the primal elements, substituting the tyrannies of a time out of joint. We see no reason why the inhabitants of our little valley should not pioneer again, now toward restoring harmony between our species and the rest of the living world. Perhaps we have more to lose, though fewer to lose it. After the Bicentennial celebrations ended, we still had a wild bear and a doe deer walk undisturbed through town. A magnificent moose with a full rack of antlers crashed through the night in the adjacent river valley, recorded only by the policemen in a prowl car.

The Paul Bunyan tree and its companions in the woodland have been set aside as a sanctuary area. The particular tract in which it stands even supports a legend: that here the planks were cut to build the historic ship *Ranger,* which was captained by John Paul Jones during the Revolution. It is a fact, not a legend, that otters make trails through the snow in the same woodland every winter, and that a bobcat comes to sharpen its claws on a big beech. The marks remind us of what we possess in the valley. They reassure us of what the heritage can be for years to come.

L.J.M. and M.M.

Index